Business Take-over
&
The Role of Financial Institutions in India

Business Take-over & The Role of Financial Institutions in India

MALAY K. ROY

Academic Foundation
☆ DELHI ☆

First Published : 1991 by

Academic Foundation

24 - A, Sriram Road, Civil Lines, Delhi - 110 054. (INDIA).

Phone : 232966, 2911852 & 233730.

BUSINESS TAKE-OVER AND
THE ROLE OF FINANCIAL INSTITUTIONS IN INDIA
by Malay K. Roy

ISBN-81-7188-020-7

Laser-Typeset & Printed by:

COMPRINT INDIA

24 - A, Sriram Road, Civil Lines, Delhi - 110 054.

Contents

Publisher's Note....

We are glad to present, in book-form, this analytical economic study on an important topical subject in the context of our present-day business and industrial climate of the country.

While this intensive study was financially supported by the Indian Council of Social Science Research, the author had sent copies of the first draft of this study to the various eminent scholars belonging to such institutions as the Reserve Bank of India; Industrial Development Bank of India; the Indian Institute of Management, Ahmedabad; the Indian Institute of Management, Calcutta; the Indian Institute of Public Administration; important Chambers of Commerce and Industry; and the professors of Business and Management Studies at the Universities of Delhi, Calcutta, Burdwan, Lucknow and North Bengal. The valuable suggestions received from the learned professors and the experts in the field, were incorporated by the author in the final version of the study that was submitted for publication.

We hope Dr. M.K. Roy's pains-taking study proves of real value and use to various institutions, business and industry establishments and the teachers and students of business and management studies at the various universities and business schools.

— Raj Kapila, *Director*,

Academic Foundation

Preface

In the last few decades Indian corporate sector has undergone considerable changes. Most important among these is the change in the shareholding pattern in favour of government controlled financial institutions. It has altered the very complexion of the private corporate sector to such an extent that it is difficult now a days to make any distinction between public and private corporate sector.

In search of a befitting role, along with these changes in shareholding pattern, institutions have also redefined the role of nominee directors on several occasions. Still now there is an unresolved controversy regarding the definition of "befitting role" and the root of this debate breeds in the basic philosophy of Mixed economy followed by the government.

Present study follows the stand that change in the shareholding pattern and thereby the power structure of the corporation *per se* has little relevance unless this change has its developmental implications. Precisely, the issue may be restated in this way - is there any possibility that this change is affecting the efficiency of the firm? Depending on the answer of the question, the issues follow : what role institutions under the circumstances should play in the corporate sector? In a sense, this study follows the stand that the role of financial institutions in the corporate sector in general and, in the context of take-over in particular, should be primarily guided by the objective of efficiency.

With this view in mind, different statistical tools and techniques have been applied to show the relationship between institutional holding and corporate economic behaviour. More specifically, the following issues are investigated in detail : is the corporate efficiency in any way related with the institutional equity holding? How the firms having high institutional holding are performing, etc. Mainly on the basis of the findings of the empirical study, the role of the institutions in the corporate sector as well as in take-over situation has been defined accordingly. Only criteria that has been considered while defining the role of institutions is its implication on the development process of our economy.
The study has been enriched by the critical comments and valuable suggestions made by Professor S.K. Goel of Indian Institute of Public Administration, Professor P.K. Ghose, Ex-Vice-Chancellor of North Bengal University, Professor S.K. Chakraborty of Indian Institute of Management, Calcutta, Professor A.K. Sarkar, Head, Department of Management Studies, Calcutta University, Professor B. Banerjee, Dean, Faculty of Commerce, Calcutta University, Professor P. Das and Professor P. Chattopadhya of Burdwan University.

Sri Mukul Saha, Lecturer, St. Joseph's College, Darjeeling, helped me in different stages of the work through his ceaseless effort without whose help and assistance the work could not have been completed.

I am also grateful to Sri Tapan Gupta and Sukhoranjan Sarkar, Assistant Librarian of North Bengal University, Officers Staff of Indian Institute of Management, Calcutta and M.R.T.P. Commission Library for making available all library facilities needed for the work. For excellent and skillful typing I thank Sri Rathin Saha and Chandan Roy. I am grateful to Sri Chitta Nai and Apurba Roy who rendered invaluable assistance in computational and data processing work.

My colleagues of the department along with Sri S.K. Chaudhuri of M.D.I., Shankar Sen Gupta of Burdwan University, Sri S. Basu and R. Bhattacharya of economics department of North Bengal University were continuous source of inspiration of my work.

I am also indebted to Indian Council of Social Science Research for the financial assistance provided by them for the completion of the work.

Last bust not the least, I am grateful to my wife Mrs. Srabani Roy who not only maintained balance between academic and social pleasure, but also absolved me of my family responsibilities during the course of this work.

— *Malay Kanti Roy*

Department of Commerce
University of North Bengal

List of Tables

CHAPTER 4

Introduction

The growth of corporate bodies breeds a complex relationship between ownership and control in an industrial sector. There are cases where owners directly manage their firms and these two functions are inseparable. In contrast to it, there are examples of complete separation of ownership from management. The corporate bodies where ownership is diffused over a large number of shareholders, the management is controlled by a small coterie formed out of them. Though they enjoy insignificant voting right, they manage business on a continual basis even ignoring real owners of the business who are disorganised, owe little stake and interest in the venture concerned.

However, the above description fails to explain the development of Indian corporate scenarios. Here the financial institutions are found holding larger shares in the corporations with a declared principle (incorporated in the spirit of mixed economy) not to indulge in direct management. The management responsibility is, therefore, necessarily vested on small shareholders. The blessings of the financial institution, however, determine who, among the small shareholders, would be entrusted with this task.

Whatever be the politico-economic values behind this development, it entrusts financial institutions with a crucial economic task viz. efficient use of resources which is normally performed by the market forces. The basic objective of this research is to assess the role of financial institutions in this regard. Before entering into the domain of research, it would be in order to review in brief the actual position of the financial institutions in India's corporate sector, and also its developmental implications.

1.1 Indian Scenario at a Glance

In the last few decades Indian corporate sector has undergone considerable changes. Most important among these, is the change in the shareholding pattern in favour of government controlled financial institutions. It has altered the very complexion of the private corporate sector to such an extent that it is difficult nowadays to make any distinction between public and private corporate sector.

Surveys conducted by Reserve Bank of India in 1959, 1965 and 1978 provide an excellent insight regarding the process of change of ownership of shares in joint stock companies. In a sense, it is a study of the evolution of power structure of corporate sector that is helpful for an understanding as to how these institutions ultimately emerged as the largest shareholder of corporate sector? What is the present state of relationship between the actual owner and the management of an Indian firm? and what are the developmental implications of these changes?

TABLE 1.1

Change of Ownership of Shares in India

Category of Owners	*1959*	*1965*	*1978*
1. Individuals	52.1	44.1*	37.3*
2. Trustees and Charitable Institutions	1.2	1.3	1.2
3. Nominee Companies	39.6	13.0	13.8*
4. Institutions and others**	7.1	20.3	27.4
5. Overseas (Individual and Institutions)	-	21.3	20.3
Total	100.0	100.0	100.0

The striking feature that emerges from the above table is the continuous rise in the proportion of shareholding of financial institutions with a corresponding decline in the shares held by individuals. The report on changes in shareholding pattern in Indian industries was published by Reserve Bank of India in 1983, and thereafter no further information on the present state of condition is available. However, if one considers the trend of capital market condition that shows some exceptional behaviour in the last few years, it would not be unrealistic to believe that in the meantime situation has further changed in favour of financial institutions. Underwriting, direct subscriptions, exercise of conversion option stipulated in loan agreements with the borrowing companies, acquisition of Rights and Bonus shares, direct market operations, are the various means used by institutions to acquire shares in a large number of companies.

Though the average equity holding of financial institutions is 27 per cent, both in the case of large companies and newly established companies, it is far above the average. It shows that greater the need for capital more is the involvement of financial institutions and this dependence is on the increase. This is the natural outcome of a situation that is partly attributable to government policies that provide different incentives and tax concessions for investment in U.T.I., L.I.C. etc. Thus a sizeable proportion of individual savings is diverted to investment institutions instead of stock market which happens to be a major partner of capital market. Along with this, different structural and other lacunas inherent in Indian economy as identified by Patel Committee[1] do not permit stock market to play its desired role in the corporate sector. As a result, these financial institutions appeared as a savior of corporate sector in terms of supply of funds and the whole process helped in gradual

---

Source : RBI Bulletin, February, 1983, p. 91.

Notes : * Excludes holdings of foreign shareholders which are included against item 5.

** It includes all State and National Level Institutions.

rise of institutional equity holding.

Industrywise analysis broadly indicates that the financial institutions had impressive shareholding in all types of industries. The rate varies from industry to industry, it is lowest in the case of Tea Plantation (15.1%) and highest in paper and paper products (39.59%). This variation mainly depends on the nature of industry, such as it is highest in the case of capital and technology intensive industries and lowest in traditional industries. Recognising this variation, the institution can be treated as a formidable force in corporate power structure even in the industry where their holding is minimum. This network of equity holding over a cross section of industries puts financial institutions into a pivotal position in the development process of the economy. They can use this power to control and guide the activities of business corporations so as to ensure best utilisation of vast economic resources invested in this sector.

It is obvious, any equity holding of more than 50 per cent permits any individual or group to retain control over a company. In modern corporations where shareholding is highly diffused, any holding even far less than 50 per cent, might be considered sufficient for control purpose. It is difficult to determine precisely any cut off rate in this regard. The rate will vary from case to case depending on the distribution pattern of shareholding of firms. However, the fact is that the greater the size of equity holding more is the scope of gaining absolute control over the firm.

Thus, from the point of view of control, the important factor is the distribution pattern of equity holding of financial institutions in the assisted companies. The reason is, if the total investment is unevenly distributed, such as small holding in a large number of companies and very big in few cases, the average may be high but the scope of effective control over companies becomes limited. So any discussion on the size of equity holding of various types of investors would be in order, to understand the relative importance of each category of investors in the corporate power structure.

In the Indian corporate sector, practically, there are two classes of shareholders - large and small. Large shareholders contribute near about 70 per cent of the total equity capital of the companies. It also implies shareholding is highly concentrated in Indian industries.

On the other hand, a large number of small shareholders, who are scattered and disorganised, contribute 27 per cent in the total equity capital of companies. Thus, small shareholders have little significance in corporate power structure, it is the large shareholders alone who matter.

Category-wise analysis of equity investment further shows that the holding of financial institutions, almost in every case, is large and they can be treated as big shareholders having considerable influence in the corporate power structure. Joint stock company is another class of investor whose holding is also very large in each case.

In contrast, small shareholders contribute near about 72 per cent of the total subscription of individual investment and big shareholders share is 21 per cent only. When the total contribution of individual shareholders' in the risk capital of the company is 38 per cent, out of which 21 per cent is supplied by large shareholders, their contribution in the total equity capital comes to as low as 8 per cent. These are the people who manage the company on behalf of a vast number of shareholders be it small or large. The small shareholder, by definition, has little stake and therefore little interest in the corporation. Among the big investors, tacit support of institutions and successful operation of the technique of intercorporate investment, help these people to remain at the helm of corporate power structure on a continual basis.

The change in the shareholding pattern, and thereby power structure of the corporation per se, has little relevance unless this change has its developmental implications. Precisely, the issue may be restated in this way — is there any possibility of this change affecting the efficiency of firms? Depending on the answer of the question, the issue follows - whether there is any need to change the attitude of institutions towards corporate sector?

To answer the above questions, at the outset, it is necessary to explore the present state of relationship between the management and ownership of firms. In India, those who manage firms own insignificant equity capital and under no stretch of imagination, they can be identified as the "owner" of the business who enjoys the right "to select or change" the management. The institutions, by virtue of their large equity-holding can be described as the real "owner" in its true sense of terms but they abstain themselves from taking part in the direct management of the corporation. Thus, there is a separation of ownership from management.

Upto this stage, the Indian situation resembles closely that of the industrially developed countries where the board holds one to two per cent of equity.[2] But in those countries the saving institutions and the financial intermediaries belong to the private sector having a close relation with big industrial houses. Moreover, shares are widely dispersed among a variety of insurance companies, banks, mutual trusts, housing societies, etc. where a concerted voting is hardly to be expected. It allows management, with insignificant equity holding, to enjoy effective control over firms and to function free from shareholders' influence. However, indirect influence of these intermediaries on corporate performance cannot be ignored. Institutions that operate in the private sector with some specific economic goal, continually reshuffle their portfolio and invest their funds from less to more remunerative outlets. Through this process, it performs an important economic function of efficient allocation and utilisation of resources. It also provides a constant pressure on existing management to improve the corporate efficiency.

In contrast to the above scenario, shareholding is highly concentrated with government controlled institutions in India. But the economic philosophy pursued by the government that is breeded in the mixed economy, forced institutions to play an indifferent role towards the corporate sector. Hence, the management even after ignoring the real owners, can manage the firms and function free from dominant shareholders' influence. Thus, in India also, like developed countries, ultimate relationship between management and ownership remains unaltered. In both the cases there is separation of ownership from management. Under the situation, where the management functions free from the shareholders' influence, they might be tempted to pursue goals that will satisfy their own interest to the exclusion of owners. The probability of "Managerial exploitation of owners" is higher in Indian situation where even the scope of indirect control by institutions according to the model of developed countries as described above is limited. In a narrow stock market that is overwhelmingly dominated by institutions, scope of continuous reshuffling of portfolio and thereby disciplining the management is minimum. Where management functions free from any direct or indirect influence of major shareholders the possibility of managerial disfunctioning and careless use of resources increases.

Further, the increase in institutional equity holding is associated with another development that might have some impact on the efficiency of the firm. The predominance of institutional investors in the Indian capital market, in turn, denotes insignificant role of stock market as a supplier of funds. Nowadays, it can supply hardly 10 per cent of the total needed funds of the private corporate sector.[3] When the dependence of the firm on the stock market is minimum, it loses its significance as an "efficient allocator of resources" and 'guardian of efficiency' which are the two major economic functions of a stock market.[4]

An inactive stock market not only induces firms to depend on institutional funds, but also encourages them to rely more on internal savings for growth and development.[5] In a developing economy, this is obviously a praiseworthy trend. But the experience of industrially developed countries leads to a confusion whether this dependence is deliberate or forced by market constraint. There is a purposeful attempt in industrially developed countries, where stock market is sufficiently active, to generate maximum funds internally.[6] The probable reason for this type of behaviour is that it allows firms to avoid capital market discipline. Management enjoys wider discretion over the use of their funds and can take decisions ignoring its repercussions on the stock market. In India, the truth is, either under compulsion or by design, by depending too much on internal savings and institutional funds, firms have been able to avoid capital market discipline to a large extent. Under the situation, the possibility of non-optimum utilisation of resources cannot be ignored.

Thus, change in the shareholding pattern, not only altered the power structure of the corporation but it also has some direct implications on the corporate efficiency. The Institution that emerged as one of the main forces of corporate power structure, has a definite role to play under the changed situation to ensure best utilisation of huge resources invested in the corporate sector. In search of a befitting role, along with these changes in shareholding pattern, institutions have also redefined the role of nominee directors on several occasions. Till now there is an unresolved controversy regarding the definition of "befitting role" and the root of this debate breeds in the basic philosophy of mixed economy followed by the government.

1.1(a) Present Debate - Need for Future Guidelines

It is often argued that to promote efficiency, to ensure better utilisation of public funds and to have a greater control on the private sector, financial institutions should play an active role in the management of the corporations. The day when the bill for establishing the Industrial Development Bank of India was passed, the then Finance Minister T.T. Krishnamacharya opined "with the establishment of more such banks, all big business would become borrowers from government and government would be able to discipline them".[7] It requires that the nominee directors have to play the role of watch dogs in the assisted companies to make sure the best possible use of the public money. If the existing management cannot utilise the resources entrusted to them efficiently, financial institutions would not hesitate to replace them by an "efficient" one. Only this type of constant threat on the existing management can improve the efficiency of corporations that are otherwise inefficient. Datta Committee (1970)[8] advanced almost the same view mentioned above. It recommended that the public financial institutions should progressively participate in management and control of assisted enterprises so as to ensure public interest. Further, "Committee to Examine the Principles of a Possible Shift from Physical to Financial control"[9] provided broad guidelines regarding the role of institutions in the private sector. It suggested that the role of institutions in the corporate sector should be guided primarily by the objective of efficiency and in the context of take-over also the objectives to be followed. In a sense, the committee favoured both corrective and punitive action on the part of the institutions to restore economic efficiency of the private sector.

The above line of thinking draws from the idea that government must be at the helm of all economic activities so as to achieve planned economic development. The objective cannot be achieved without any effective control over corporate sector. The views expressed get further momentum from the fact that the management of Indian corporations function free from the influence of individual investors, stock market discipline and capital market constraint at large. It requires direct intervention of institutions to discipline corporate management that is otherwise inefficient.

There are equally strong counter arguments also. In a mixed economy the private corporate sector has a definite role to play. Any interference by government controlled financial institutions in the management of corporation will go against the very essence of mixed economy. The Memorandum submitted by F.I.C.C.I. to Narasimham committee emphasises this aspect. It highlights the need for "competitive efficiency", "independence of management", protection against any move to "destabilise existing management" etc. Practically, while dealing with the issue of role of nominee directors, memorandum concludes that already there is enough monitoring on corporations by other government agencies and therefore, the financial institutions should not duplicate their function. The argument goes further that the existing controls and regulations should be reviewed and the "normal laws of economics" should be given the chance to operate.

The underlying spirit of this type of argument is that the government should bloom the corporate sector by providing funds, subsidies, protection but restrain themselves from interfering in the management of the corporations. Utter failure of different types of physical and financial controls and their adverse impact on the development of corporate sector, is often cited as an example in support of this argument. Thus, the logic follows, institutional interference in the management of corporation, instead of improving, will be instrumental in further deterioration of the existing situation. Interestingly, when it is believed that any sort of institutional control is detrimental to corporate efficiency, the operation of market economy in its true sense of the term is also not favoured.

In view of this conflicting assertion it is necessary to develop a well defined guideline regarding the role of financial institutions in the private corporate sector and the principles to be followed by the institutions in the context of take-over. It is felt that there is the necessity to develop a guiding principle which would operate under a set of well understood rules without the necessity of intervention in individual cases. The present study is an attempt in this direction.

1.2 Scope of the Study

The study under consideration is basically empirical in nature. The principle purpose of the empirical analysis is to investigate the effect of separation of ownership from control on the performance of the firms. This is the situation that clearly exists in India. On the other hand, the study will be helpful for an understanding whether the rise in institutional equity holding and their present attitude towards corporate sector is in any way related with the efficiency of the firm. The findings of the study will help to develop policies based on economic criteria to be followed by the institutions in the private sector, specially in the context of take-over. In a sense the present study follows the stand that the role of financial institutions in the private corporate sector should be guided primarily by the objective of efficiency.

Pioneering work of Berle and Means[10] inspired scores of researchers to study economic implications of separation of ownership from control. Most of the studies are based on U.K. and U.S. experiences. Methodology, time period, number of variables considered vary widely in different studies. Such as Kamerschen, 1968,[11] Larner, 1966,[12] Radice, 1971,[13] Peter Holl, 1975,[14] considered only two variables such as profitability and growth and tried to examine whether management control exerts any significant influence on these variables. Study of Sorensen, 1974[15] is slightly different, in the sense that it considered five variables instead of two as in the earlier studies and examined the goals "owner controlled" and "management controlled" firms tried to pursue. Study of McEachern, 1978[16] is more relevant in the context of present work. He identified three groups of firms viz. owner controlled, management controlled, externally controlled firms and tried to show the relationship between control type and growth. The study is more practical, in the sense, it considered in greater details the complex relationship between management and ownership of the firm and attempted to measure the efficiency consequences arising out of it. Study of Thonet and Poensgen, 1979[17] is the only exception as it highlights German experiences of separation of ownership from control. Apart from these studies, there are also a number of empirical studies of similar nature that have been avoided for the purpose of discussions.

All the above mentioned studies primarily tried to test the hypothesis of Berle and Means (1934)[18] that owner and management control firm would try to pursuit different goals. The findings of the studies are inconclusive. Undoubtedly the studies are interesting, thought provocative and will draw attention of researchers in their own right.

The problems with these studies are, firstly, most of the studies are based on the experiences of industrially developed countries and the findings may have little relevance in the Indian context. The pattern of shareholding, a unique role of institutions and the overall economic setting in which Indian corporate sector operates make all the differences. Secondly, different 'cut off' points have been used in different studies to define management control. Even the studies based on the experience of a particular country adopted different definition for "management" and 'owner' control firm. Lastly, most of the studies are based on the time period 1948 to 1967, as a result recent experiences of industrially developed countries are also not available.

The main thrust of the present study deviates significantly from the studies mentioned earlier though there are some common points of interest. The present study restricts itself to those empirical questions which are directly related to the issue of role of financial institutions in the private corporate sector and to certain other aspects directly connected with it. With this objective in mind, the comparative economic and financial characteristics of the management control firms[19] are systematically analysed and in particular the following empirical questions are discussed in varying degrees of detail.

Firstly, given the economic and financial records of firms, to what extent, if at all, is it possible to discriminate between management control firms and others?

Secondly, considering the same economic and financial records whether it is possible to discriminate among management control firms having different degrees of equity holding of financial institutions?

Thirdly, institutional holding to what extent, if at all, can influence the corporate economic behaviour?

Though these three issues are quite independent but they are closely related with one another and have a direct bearing with the main policy issue discussed earlier. The first and second questions try to measure the effect of huge institutional holding on the performance of the firm and the third tries to show the relationship between institutional holding and corporate economic behaviour. These issues again are directly related with the stand of the present thesis that the role of financial institutions in the private corporate sector should be guided by the objective of efficiency.

Lastly, attempt will also be made to study - is it possible to identify any specific goal that management control firm attempts to achieve in exclusion of others? Practically the last issue has little relevance so far as the basic policy question of the present theme is concerned. Obviously, not only it will help for a better understanding of the behaviour of the firm with the change in institutional holding but also to test the hypothesis of "Managerial theory" in the Indian context.

Four basic variables have been used for the purpose of the analysis. Two variables, pretax rate of return on net assets, and growth, mainly measure efficiency of the firm, whereas valuation ratio and return on equity measure a firm's efficiency in terms of its supplier of equity fund. Detailed description of the variables will be provided in the chapter which follows. The results of the empirical analysis, apart from their intrinsic interest, bear directly on the policy issue described earlier.

Though the basic issue "role of financial institutions in the private corporate sector" has a far reaching economic implications, it failed to draw serious attention of the researchers. It appears from certain very casual writings here and there that hardly deserve any attention. Though the approach of L.C. Gupta is different, he systematically tried to develop certain guiding principles to redefine the role of nominee directors. It appears that L.C. Gupta[21] avoided the basic issue, to what extent, if at all, it is necessary for financial institutions to control the affairs of the private corporate sector? Once this basic issue is resolved then only the role of nominee directors, and its approach towards take-over can be defined accordingly. It is expected that the present empirical investigation, that wholly depends on economic criteria in exclusion of others, may be helpful in this process. It is worthwhile to mention that the basic issue under consideration is very broad and complicated. Any conclusion based on economic criteria alone may be misleading. It is believed that the present exercise may only help in the process of development of an informed opinion on a hotly debated issue of the recent time.

1.3 The Data Used

The study is based on three main kinds and sources of information. Firstly, and by far the most important, are the standardised accounting data on quoted firms prepared by the Bombay Stock Exchange. This source has been applied for the collection of data regarding the economic performance of the sample companies.

Secondly, another major data source is R.B.I. Bulletin. Mainly macro economic information have been collected from this source. Thirdly, equity holding of financial institutions in the companies under studies have been collected from the working paper no. - 17,[21] prepared by Prof. S.K. Goel of Indian Institute of Public Administration. This is supplemented by further data available in Economic Times. Apart from the above three major sources, the study depends upon different government and non-government publications.

1.4 Plan of the Study

The central purpose of chapter 2 is to discuss the general conception, the broad issues to which it is related and the nature of the data used. As it is felt necessary to introduce the sample companies in greater details and to discuss the theoretical justifications and intricacies of the variables used to measure the economic efficiency of sample firms, the whole of the second chapter is devoted for this purpose.

In Chapters 3 and 4 the economic and financial characteristics of the management controlled firms are compared with that of others. The analysis of chapters 3 and 4 is done on a univariate and multivariate basis.

Chapter 5 mainly deals with the policy implications of the study which is based on main empirical conclusions of Chapters 3 and 4. Some other aspects, which are also directly or indirectly related with the main theme of the study, have also been considered here.

It may be noted that the main conclusions - especially the main empirical conclusions - are normally summarised at the end of each chapter. Although all the qualifications to the conclusions cannot be given in the summaries, they may be found useful for cross reference purpose as well as for giving a brief abstract of what is contained in the chapter.

NOTES AND REFERENCES

1. See, Report of High Powered Committee on Stock Exchange Reforms under the chairmanship of Mr. G.S. Patel.
2. Robin Marris, The Economic Theory of Managerial Capitalism, Macmillan Company, London, 1964, p. 17.
3. The estimate is based on the Report of Rangarajan Committee.
4. W.G. Baumol, The Stock Market and Economic Efficiency, New York, 1965, pp. 35-37.
5. Internal savings provide nearly 51 per cent of the total needed funds of private sector. It includes both depreciation and retained profit. If depreciation is excluded, internal savings provide nearly 19 per cent of the funds required by private sector (See Rangarajan Committee Report).
6. Gordon Donaldson, Corporate Debt Capacity, Boston, 1961, p. 39. Simon Kuznets, Capital in the American Economy; Its Formation and Financing, Princeton University Press, 1961, Singh and Whittington, Growth, Profitability and valuation, Cambridge, 1968, pp. 39-45.

7. Thanyavur, Companies Act Amendment Bill, Economic and Political Weekly, December, 26th 1987, p. 2247.

8. Industrial Licensing Policy Enquiry Committee (1969) Report, New Delhi, Paras 2; 17; 7; 90 and 8; 18.

9. Committee to Examine the Principles of a Possible Shift from Physical to Financial Control, appointed by the Ministry of Finance under the chairmanship of Narasimham.

10. Berle and Means, The Modern Corporation and Private Property, Macmillan, New York, 1932.

11. D.R. Kamerschen, "The Influence of Ownership and Control on Profit Rates" American Economic Review, Vol. 58, (1968), p. 432.

12. R.J. Larner, "Ownership and Control in the 200 Largest Non-Financial Corporations, 1929 and 1963", American Economic Review, September, 1966, 56, pp. 777-87.

13. H.K. Radice, "Control Type, Profitability and Growth in Large Firms: An Empirical Study", The Economic Journal, Vol. 81, September, 1971, pp. 547-561.

14. Peter Holl, "Effect on Control Type on the Performance of the Firm in the U.K.", The Journal of Industrial Economics, Vol. XXIII, June 1975, pp. 257-271.

15. Robert Sorensen, "The Separation of Ownership and Control and Firm Performance" Southern Economic Journal, Vol. 41 (1974) July, pp. 145-143.

16. William McEachern, "Corporate Control and Growth : An Alternative Approach" The Journal of Industrial Economics, March, 1978, pp. 257-266.

17. Thonet and Poensgen, "Managerial Control and Economic Performance in Western Germany", The Journal of Industrial Economics, September, 1979, pp. 23-27.

18. Berle and Means, op. cit., 1932.

19. It denotes the firms where financial institutions by virtue of their large equity holding is the real owner of the business but they are managed by others. Detailed discussion on this issue has been made in the next chapter.

20. L.C. Gupta, "Nominee Directors' Role and Impact", M.D.I. Management Journal, Vol. I, No. 1, January, 1988, pp. 39-52. Corporate Management and Accountability : Towards a Joint Sector, Macmillan India, Specially Ch. 4.

21. S.K. Goel, "Private Management and Take-overs of Public Owned Companies - Some Issues for Debate", Working Paper No. 17, I.I.P.A., May 1983.

Variables, Sample and Time Period of Study

Introduction

Measurement of efficiency of firms to study the implications of separation of ownership from control require identification of proper objectives that are expected to be achieved by the firms. It will help to identify the variables that would be proper to use for efficiency measurement purposes. In view of conflicting assertions regarding theories of the firm, the task becomes complicated. It is not the principal objective of the study to prove correctness of one theory over another. Keeping in mind the Indian situations, elements of different theories are combined to provide a range of performance criteria which will be used to measure the economic significance of separation of ownership from control. Obviously, the process of study will also help in an indirect way to identify any specific objective that a management control firm may desire to achieve.

Further, it is also necessary to provide clarification of the "cut off" point that is used to identify a firm as management controlled. It is specially important because different rates were used without providing any scientific reason in different studies conducted in industrially developed countries while differentiating between management controlled and owner controlled firm.[1] In the Indian context it is specially necessary to develop a definition to identify the situation where there is separation of ownership from control.

This section mainly deals with three issues :

(a) Theoretical justifications for selecting certain variables to measure efficiency of management controlled firms and detailed description of those variables.

(b) Justification for using different cut off points to define management controlled firm.

(c) Detailed description of sample firms, problems that might arise while dealing with this sample in the empirical study and the process by which the problems have been dealt with.

2.1 Theories of the Firm

Economists have long expressed dissatisfaction with the neo-classical assumption concerning the managers single minded pursuit of profit. Over the past two decades several alternative theories of the firm have been formalized, all suggesting that in the absence of strict product market or capital market constraints, managers pursue goals other than profits. A common thread among these "managerial" theories is that managers are interested in the power, salary, status and non-pecuniary benefits that come with firm size and growth and argue that managers attempt to maximize firm growth subject to some minimum performance constraint. Marris, for example, contended management control firm would plough back profit to sustain growth rate of the firm, ultimately causing decrease in marginal rate of return on new investment below the cost of capital, resulting in efficiency loss in the management control firm. Among others, the present study takes Marris[2] version of the managerial theory of the firm as its starting point, critically analyzes it and provides an alternative hypothesis regarding theories of the firm suited for the Indian condition.

2.1(a) Managerial Theory of Firm

In the theory of managerial capitalism developed by Marris there are two functional relationships contained in the profit rate/growth rate plane; these are the demand growth curve and the supply of capital curve shown diagrammatically below.

DIAGRAM — 1

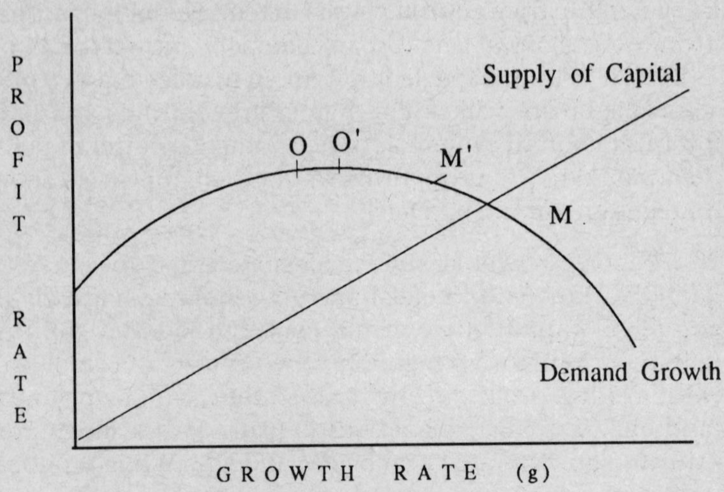

If owners' utility is maximized by maximizing profitability (Profit rate) they will select the combination of P and g represented by the point O. This assumes, however, that all capital gains are realized. If this is not the case, the combination chosen will be to the right of O on the demand growth curve, say O'. At this point also, the valuation ratio is maximized. Managers, however, when wanting to maximize their own utility function are assumed to maximize growth and will therefore aim for the combination of p and G given by the point M. But they will also be subject to constraint in their choice because their desire for growth must be matched by at least a minimum level of security price as represented by the valuation ratio. Thus managers will choose a combination of p and g to the left of M on the demand growth curve say M.' At this point the valuation ratio is not maximized. Indeed, the point chosen depends upon the extent to which the valuation ratio acts as a constraint on managerial action - in short, on the extent to which the stock market conforms to Neo-classical assumptions. The choice open to the firm, then, lies on negatively sloped part of the demand growth curve between O and M. Moreover, if the separation of ownership from control results in management being able to take decisions at least in part, independently of the shareholder, it is to be expected that on an average management controlled firms will exhibit higher growth rates and lower profit rates than owner controlled firms. A scatter of points relating P and G across firms would then appear as shown in diagram 2 (on next page).

The scatter would show a positive trend (because the larger variations in the demand growth curve, vis a vis the supply of capital curve would identify the latter) with the points forming two subgroups, one for owner control firms with average profit rate and growth rate given by po and go and one for management control firms with average profit rate and growth rate given by PM and GM. While profit rate is measured as the sum of annual pretax profit for the relevant time period divided by aggregate net assets for the same period. The growth rate is measured as the growth of net assets compounded annually.

Above discussions, in a very simple way, show how manager controlled firms, which are viewed as being operated in the interests of managers instead of stock holders, are expected to behave in terms of two variables growth and profitability. However if the elements of different managerial theories are combined together, following hypothesis regarding the behaviour of management controlled firms can

DIAGRAM — 2

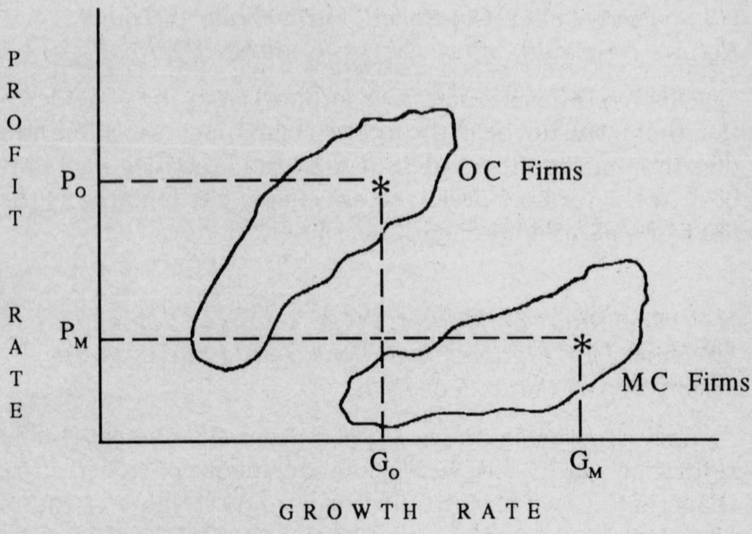

be developed :

H1 : Management Controlled Firms Grow Faster than Owner Controlled Firms

Utility function of owner and manager is different, management will emphasize on growth than on profit that will help for the satisfaction of their own goal in terms of power, prestige, perquisites etc.

H2 : Rate of Return on Management Controlled Firms will be Lower than Owner Controlled Firms

Since managers do not reap the profits of the firm they

will not make profit their primary goals - unless induced to do so by means of appropriate, mainly monetary incentives or are forced to do so, either by the market or by the imminent danger of concerted action of the owners to remove them from their job.

H3 : Management Controlled Firms have a Lower Return on Equity than Owner Controlled Firms

This hypothesis also draws support from the consideration that it will not be in the interest of managers to show and distribute all profits made but to spend (and disguise) part of it in the form of preferred expenses, particularly in the form of staff and managerial perquisites.

H4 : The Ratio of Market Value to Book Value will be Lower for Management Controlled Firm than it is for Owner Controlled Firm

This hypothesis draws support from H3. Hence, rate of return on equity is lower in management controlled firm, than that of owner controlled firm, market value of equity and thereby market value to book value ratio will also be lower.

The above mentioned hypothesis are not exhaustive that can be developed from a careful study of the managerial theory but primary in nature. Empirical studies based on managerial theory neither accept nor reject the above mentioned hypothesis, findings are contradictory that is inconclusive.[5]

However, it is contended, actual behaviour of manager, that is priority they will place for the satisfaction of their own goal in terms of power, prestige, perquisites that can be achieved through growth depends upon nature and extent of control mechanism available to check the activities of manager. Availability of sound control mechanism can only ensure proper utilisation of scarce resources and protection of the interest of real owners. Issues have been dealt with in the latter section.

2.1(b) Take-over - Managerial Theory and Efficiency of Firm

In the above general framework actual behaviour of managers will be highly influenced by the role of stock market and corporate control market.[6] The market for corporate control is concerned with the relationship between the market value of a company's common stock and value of the assets to which it relates. If the former is divided by the latter, valuation ratio is obtained. It provides an index showing how rewarding it would be for an outside interest to purchase control of a company - other things being equal, the lower the ratio the more profitable the purchase. Management which is not maximising returns to the owners of the company will find this fact reflected in a lower common share price. As the market value of equity falls in relation to the value of physical assets (i.e. as the valuation ratio falls) it may become advantageous for an outside party to purchase those shares and, with them, control of the company. If this market is fully efficient, management cannot do anything but maximize returns to owners, as the only alternative is to forfeit corporate control. Thus an efficient stock market along with a market for corporate control can ensure proper utilization of resources entrusted to the manager and to protect the interest of general investors.[7]

It would further prevent management from making excessive preferred expenses, particularly in the form of staff and managerial perquisites that might adversely affect the profitability of the firm. J.E. Meade[8] sums up the argument on this point as follows - "A company which sacrifices profit either to an easy life or to unprofitable growth makes itself liable to take-over bid. Suppose that the management of a large concern has become slack in the sense that it is not effectively selling the product for which consumers are prepared to pay most or it is not cutting its costs of production most efficiently; or suppose that the management of the concern is sacrificing profit to growth by using funds to finance the company's growth, even though this is a relatively unprofitable form of business" - in all these cases market value of shares and thereby valuation ratio will decrease and the company will be subject to take-over. There will be "replacement of the management by one which is more efficient or profit minded and could increase the market value of the company's shares. It may well be true that the ordinary shareholders dispersed throughout society will not in fact be able to get together to enforce such a change. But a generous bid for the company's shares on the part of some other large company or institution may enable a majority of the shares to be acquired by a single institutional owner which can enforce the change of management, increase thereby the value of the company's share and thus reap a large benefit".

In practice the whole issue is not as simple as it has been described above. The approach depends heavily on the efficient functioning of the stock market, the market that can evaluate the share properly depending on the future earning potentiality of the firm under existing management. This can provide a reliable signal about the firm whose assets are not properly utilised under existing management and inspire others to take-over management of the firm at a low price prevailing in the market. Although there are differing views, there is a good deal of evidence that the prices yielded by the stock markets in the real situation are very far from such an ideal. This evidence indicates that apart from the inevitable ignorance of the future, share prices are much influenced by unequal availability of information, speculation and by many other market imperfections and that the capital market typically exhibits disequilibrium. If the market cannot behave properly, both in terms of the valuation of company securities and in terms of take-over mechanism referred above, it can exert little influence upon the functioning of the corporation.

It is further necessary to look after certain additional problems that prevent take-over mechanism to operate efficiently. Since a take-over is usually followed by the removal of the incumbent management, and the loss of income and perquisites associated with top managerial positions, it is a move that managers fear. Once a bid is made there are various ploys that incumbent management can pursue in an attempt to successfully reject the bid. It can raise the dividend given to shareholders in an attempt to maintain their support and drive up the price of the stock temporarily. It can purchase its own shares in the open market from those ready to sell and so reduce the amount of stock in unfriendly hands, again driving up its price. In both the cases value of the share and the cost of the take-over to the raider firm will increase and the take-over will be less attractive. Again management of the targeted company can encourage an enquiry into the bid by the government, if there is any possibility of it offending M.R.T.P. or FERA Act. Sometimes legal actions are taken on different grounds to create confusion and to kill time so that raider loses interest in take-over. An alert management whose company is ripe for a take-over bid, is likely to have contingency plans ready for such an event. While the existence of these plans will not guarantee that a bid will be successfully rejected, it suggests that defending management has a definite advantage over the acquisition minded firm and that take-over mechanism can be partly effective to discipline the management controlled firm.[9] These are not mere theoretical propositions. Any keen observer of fierce take-over battle for D.C.M. Escort, Shaw Wallace would reveal that all the techniques mentioned were applied in practice to resist take-over.

In India there is every reason to doubt the efficient functioning of the stock market. Moreover, corporate control market is also not that much developed. Take-over is an integral part of capitalist economy, that provides a constant threat on existing management and ensures better utilisation of resources. In India, to prevent the growth of monopoly, there are several restrictions on take-over. On the other hand it also helped existing management to function almost freely without any possible threat from their counterpart.

Under the existing situation, the behaviour of corporate manager will be dependent on the role of institutions, who by virtue of their large equity holding can take corrective and punitive[10] action against the existing management. Thus goal management control firm will pursue and the extent of possible managerial exploitation of owner will depend upon the attitude of institutions towards these corporations.

2.2 Description of Variables

The following variables were used to describe the economic and financial characteristics of management controlled firm

1) Pre tax rate of return on net assets (X1)

2) Growth of net assets (X2)

3) Return on equity (X3)

4) Valuation ratio (X4).

At the outset that it requires to be mentioned, the variables under consideration are a direct off shoot of earlier discussions. These are widely used and may also be treated as a general measure of efficiency. Moreover, selection of the variables would help to test the hypothesis of 'Managerial Theory' in the Indian context.

Further, it is to be mentioned that performance as a reflection of behaviour may be analyzed from the angle of shareholders, supplier of debt, employees, society at large etc. Recognising the need for measuring the performance of firms from a broader perspective, the present study confines itself to measuring the performance of firms from shareholders viewpoint. Apart from the above mentioned four variables there are also a large number of other variables that might be used for this purpose. As it is believed, the ultimate effect of variables that are excluded from the study is properly incorporated in the variables under consideration and so the former have been ignored.

Variable X_1 to X_3 are based on accounting data while X_4 uses both accounting data and the stock market valuation of the firm. Accounting information suffers from certain inherent drawbacks due to the present accounting practices. As the study relies on accounting data it is also not free from it. It is also a fact that accounting data, inspite of their defects, represent in most cases the best available indication to investors and shareholders about the current and past record of a firm. These are the data used and discussed in the financial press and in the financial community, generally to indicate company performance. Moreover, many accounting definitions of the same variables are possible. However, given the nature of the available data, the definitions finally selected and used here are the most appropriate both from the economic as well as the practical point of view.

Turning first to X_1, "Net assets" are defined as total fixed assets plus current assets; assets being valued, as is the usual practice in balance sheets, at historic costs net of depreciation. Profit that is considered is net income of the business before charging interest and making any provision for taxation. The variable shows productivity of the total lump of capital employed. For the purpose of the present study mean profitability for the time period has been taken into account.

Though profitability measured in terms of profit and total asset employed is widely used to indicate the efficiency of a firm, it is simultaneously subject to a wide range of criticism. It is easy to demonstrate that two firms, which have in fact the same profitability, could in principle show different accounting rates of return if their rates of growth (of the acquisition of fixed asset more accurately) are not the same. The one with higher growth rate will show lower accounting profitability and vice versa. The reason for this phenomenon is that depreciation is not accurately measured by the rules of the thumb normally employed by accountants for this purpose. Moreover, there is wide range of controversy regarding the definition of assets and profit to be considered in the ratio. The purpose of the discussion is to show that profitability as a measure of efficiency should be used with other performance measure. However, the reason for selecting this variable as a measure of efficiency in the present study is its wide application and general appeal.[11]

In relation to X_2 "growth", it should be noted that this variable measures the growth in terms of total assets employed (Fixed plus current assets) net of depreciation as opposed to long term financial capital. Growth can also be measured in terms of number of employees, sales, value added etc. Information regarding the number of employees and value added is not readily available and for this reason most of the studies depend upon sales and assets to calculate growth rate. The principle is also followed in the present study. The growth rate of assets has been calculated on compounding basis.

Variable X_3 deals with return on equity. Where equity has been defined as equity capital plus free reserve and surpluses that is often described as net worth. Return means net income that is available to equity shareholders after payment of preference dividend from the distributable profit. Dividend as a measure of return on equity has intentionally been avoided. Dividend is that part of the total earnings that is distributed to the shareholders and the rest is ploughed back in the business to be used for future growth. However, in the long run and under the condition of certainty any of the two measures can be used to measure return on equity.

The ratio may be treated as an alternative way to measure efficiency of the firm. It has been used as a measure of efficiency in many earlier studies. Though this ratio is also not free from criticism, it has an added advantage over the ratio X_1, as it suggests how efficiently capital structure of the company is managed. However, this statement is to be accepted with caution. It is easy to demonstrate that two companies identical in all respects, having the same amount of profit, one by simply using more debt in the capital structure can increase its earnings to equity under certain conditions. While using more debt may help to enhance earnings available to shareholders, the possibility of variability in earnings also increases causing rise in riskiness of the firm. As a result, some of the studies while accepting return on equity as a measure of efficiency considered it in conjunction with other variables to measure riskiness of the firm.[12] The process has not been adopted in the present study on the basis of the assumption that firms within a particular industry generally follow a pattern capital structure. Hence in the context of an industry, it is earnings to equity that is important, and issue of capital structure may be avoided.

The average value of return on equity for the time period has been considered in the study.

In respect to X_4 "valuation ratio", in the theory of finance is generally defined as "Book value to Market value" ratio. It shows the relationship between market value of a firm's common equity and the book value of its net equity assets. If assets were valued in a company's balance sheets at replacement cost, the denominator of the expression, could be regarded as a reflection of the value of the economic resources employed by the firm. The numerator on the other hand reflects the stock market's valuation of the earning power of these resources under the existing management.

Ideally the book value of share is to be calculated on the basis of replacement cost of assets. As the accounts are prepared on the basis of historical cost, book value for the present study has been calculated accordingly. Average of high and low market prices has been considered as the market value of shares. Again valuation ratio has been calculated on the basis of averaging method.

The above four variables have been used to measure the performance of management controlled firm. This is a comparative study - records of group of companies are being compared either within the group itself or with industry record. While comparing performance of sample firm with industry, industry average has been considered as standard, the information which is published in R.B.I. bulletin at an interval. As the sample firms are very big in size the performance of these firms have been compared with the record of large and medium size industry, published by R.B.I. bulletin. Acceptance of industry average as an ideal might be a subject of criticism. But the problem is, in an ideal condition what ought to be the outcome in terms of mentioned variables is difficult to measure. So industry average is considered as the minimum standard that the firms are expected to achieve.

In the case of valuation ratio only standard has been considered as 1. It has been asserted by Marris, in a well managed business this ratio must be at least 1 or above. If it is below 1, it will be subject to takeover bid, as the bidder will be able to acquire some productive assets at a price which is lower than the book value. However, the appropriateness of the logic depends heavily on the efficient functioning of the stock market. Efficient in terms of its ability to value share depending on future earning potentiality of the firm.

Having looked at the accounting definitions of the variables, it is important at this stage to see their economic implications in the context of some of the issues raised in Chapter 1. It may be recalled that one of the main issues with which the study is concerned, is the extent, if any, the performance of the management controlled firms can be distinguished from that of others. The issue has a significant bearing on the current controversy on the role of financial institutions in the private corporate sector specially in the context of takeover. The issue lies at the heart of the debate between minimum control, maximum freedom on the one hand and those who favour tighter control over private corporate sector to streamline its activities to achieve the maximum out of it. The variables that have been used in the study will help to measure the efficiency of management control firm that is directly related with the main theme of the study.

Secondly, a systematic study of the above mentioned variables will also help to identify the objective management control firms try to achieve, a secondary purpose of the study. In a sense, it would help to understand the relevance of Robin Marris proposition in the Indian context.

2.3 Definition of Management Control

In order to measure efficiency of management controlled firms, it is first necessary to establish some criterion for identifying firms as management controlled. Legally the ultimate control over the activities of the corporation is vested in the shareholders through the exercise of their votes at the annual meetings. In practice, however, it is the board of directors which monitors the activities of the firm on a continual basis. Corporate control may then be envisioned as residing in the individual or group which has the power to select and/or replace (and hence can strongly influence) the men who sit as the board of directors.

If an individual or group acting together own 50 per cent or more of the total outstanding stock, they possess the voting power to determine the composition of the board of directors and thus possess complete control of the corporation. As the stock becomes more widely dispersed among increased number of shareholders, an amount less than 50 per cent would be sufficient for maintaining control. In their pioneering study Berle and Means accepted a share concentration of 20 per cent or more, known to be held by an individual or group acting in concern, as sufficient for maintaining effective control. More recently different empirical studies based on the experience of different countries used various cut off rates to define control situation. However, in India due to the presence of certain legal criteria, it is easier to define a management control firm with lesser amount of ambiguity.

According to the Securities Contracts Regulation Act if any person or group holds 25% or more of the outstanding share of a company, then the person or group is treated as the owner of that business. Applying this definition, Government controlled financial institutions are the real owners of the business where their holding is equal to or more than

25%. The person who is controlling the business may be called "Manager".

Further, according to the Monopolies and Restrictive Trade Practices Act, 1969, one does not require more than 33.3 per cent of equity shares to qualify for being grouped under a House. If the public sector financial institutions were also treated as a House (which it is in terms of the economic interests in Industry, trade and services) all private sector companies in which the financial institutions held equity more than 33.3 per cent should be treated as under the control of institutions. Board may be treated as the 'manager' of the business functioning under the direct control of financial institutions.

Again where the holding of financial institutions is more than 50 per cent there is no ambiguity regarding the ownership of the firm. Under section 619(B) of the Companies Act, 1956, the companies in which more than 51 per cent of the equity shares are held, singly or jointly, by one or more governments and government companies or corporations have to be treated as "Deemed government companies". The status of the person controlling the business is obviously no better than a manager.

For the purpose of the present study, the definition provided by the Securities Regulation Act has been adopted to identify the real owner of the firm. Accordingly, financial institutions have been identified as the owner of the business where their equity holding is equal to or more than 25% and the persons who are controlling the business have been identified as "Manager" of the business, managing on behalf of the financial institution.

It appears that these firms have all the characteristics of 'owner controlled' firms, where owners can be identified easily and they possess sufficient amount of voting shares necessary to control the affairs of the corporations. In fact the issue is very complicated because of the peculiar Indian condition. In a number of earlier studies, owner controlled firms were defined as "owner controlled firms include both firms owned and managed by their owners and firms where ownership is divorced from management but concentrated so that owners can exert a strong influence upon management".[13] As a result some researchers believe that if firms are to be sorted based on the type of control, a more fruitful and less ambiguous division would involve three rather than two types of control; and would consist of[14] (1) owner managed firms, i.e., the firms owned and managed by owners (2) Externally controlled firms i.e. dominant stockholders are not a part of the management but 'active control' exists in the hands of external owner. Here the management is not free from dominant shareholder constraint. Representation on the board of directors or in the management of the firm is considered to be evidence of active control, (3) manager controlled firms.

Now applying the criteria provided by the Securities Contracts Regulation Act, financial institutions may be regarded as the real owner of firms where their equity holding is equal to or more than 25%. But these firms cannot be called "owner managed" firms, as the real owner i.e. financial institutions do not really manage the firms. At best these firms can be called 'externally controlled' firms. Here again the problem is, Indian experiences show that the 'managers' of these firms function almost freely from the dominant shareholders (F.I.) influence. If one considers the way the board is formed by the controlling group giving it the nature of a dummy character, representative of real owner (F.I.) in the board, the process of automatic inclusion of younger members of the controlling group in boards, financial institutions' ability and willingness to influence the management of the corporation in any situation, it will be clear that the external owner, not to speak about "strong influence", exert little influence upon the management of the corporation. Relationship between financial institutions and that of the assisted companies is defined by certain rules and the scope of exerting "strong influence" is very limited. Thus, active control in these firms actually exists with the manager of the business and not with the passive external owner. Managers in these firms perform "free from a dominant stockholder constraint" that is an essential condition for describing a firm as management control.

Thus it is a unique Indian situation that does not conform with the experiences of industrially developed countries. In those countries, the firms, where shareholding pattern is diffused and no single or group of shareholders can be identified as the real owner of the business who can exert "active control" on the management of the corporation are generally described as the management control firm. In India, real owners in the present context can be identified but the firms are described as management control - where there is separation of ownership from control. It is believed, if these firms are identified as "owner controlled" firms it would be a case of very mechanical thinking that avoids reality. It would be more realistic to consider these firms as management controlled firms. Obviously the type of management controlled firms referred above in connection with industrially developed countries exist in India. As the present study mainly deals with the role of financial institutions in the private corporate sector, economic implications of separation of ownership from control in the context of institutional owned firms have been taken into account.[15]

Further these management controlled firms have been classified into three groups -

Group I - It consists of firms where financial institution holding is equal to or more than 25 percent but less than 33.3 per cent.

Group II - It covers the firms where institutional holding is equal to or more than 33.3 per cent but less than 50 per cent.

Group III - Consists of those firms where financial institutions holding is equal to or more than 50 per cent.

It is clear that the grouping has been made according to

the different "control" definitions provided earlier. This classification will offer an opportunity to make an inter group comparison within the management controlled firm. It will also help to identify, within management controlled firms, whether performances in any way related with institutional holding.

The problem one will face while introducing the above criteria is, the firm that has been identified as management controlled at the beginning cannot be expected to remain so through out the period of the study. Considering the present capital market condition, while it is expected that the reliance of the private corporate sector on financial institutions will go on increasing, it can reasonably be assumed that there is little chance of sudden decrease in the equity holding of institutions. However, there is the possibility of misclassification among different groups within the management controlled firms. This possibility is minimized due to the fact that the range of equity holding on the basis of which different groups have been constructed is sufficiently large. Assuming there is little possibility of abrupt change in equity holding of financial institution, it can be argued that the chance of moving from one group to higher group by the firm is also minimum, excepting those cases which are at the margin of each group.

2.4 Sample

The study relies heavily on the list of companies where equity holding of financial institutions is equal to or more than 25%, provided in the working paper no. 17 and 18 by Prof. S.K. Goel of I.I.P.A. Some of the companies from these lists were ignored as the companies were not listed in the stock market and necessary information were not readily available.

Detailed description of sample firm is given on the next page:

Table 2.1

Total Sample-99 (Institutional holding equal to or more than 25%) Groupwise Classification

			% of total
Ist group	(Institutional holding equal to or more than 25% but less than 33.3%)	46	46% approx.
IInd group	(Institutional holding equal to or more than 33.3% but less than 50%)	42	43% approx.
IIIrd group	(Institutional holding equal to or more than 50%)	11	11% approx.
Total		99	100%

Classification of Firms by Industry and Group

Broad Classification	*N*		*Number in each group* 1	2	3	*Industry wise classification*			*Number in each group* 1	2	3
1. Agriculture and Allied products	1	=	1	x	x	Tea Plantation	1		1	x	x
							1		1	x	x
2. Processing and Manufacturing of Food stuff, Textile, Tobaccos, Leather and Products thereof	19	=	11	8	x	i) Cotton Textile	11	=	6	5	x
						ii) Food stuff	2	=	1	1	x
						iii) Jute Textile	2	=	1	1	x
						iv) Tobacco	1	=	1	x	x
						v) Silk Woolen Rayon Textile	3	=	2	1	x
							19	=	11	8	x
3. Processing and Manufacturing of Metals											

Broad Classification	*Number in each group*				*Industry wise classification*	*Number in each group*			
		1	*2*	*3*			*1*	*2*	*3*
Chemicals & Products thereof	41 =	18	17	6	i) Engineering	23 =	11	9	3
					ii) Chemicals	16 =	7	6	3
					iii) Aluminium	2 =	0	2	0
						41 =	18	17	6
4. Process and Manufacture not elsewhere classified	13 =	5	5	3	i) Cement	3 =	1	2	x
					ii) Paper and Paper product	9 =	3	3	3
					iii) Glass and Glassware	1 =	1	x	x
						13 =	5	5	3
5. Other Industries	25 =	11	12	2	i) Electric generation and supply	6 =	x	4	2
					ii) Trading	5 =	3	2	x
					iii) Shipping and Transportation	7 =	5	2	x
					iv) Investment	1 =	x	1	x
					v) Miscellaneous	6 =	3	3	x
						25 =	11	12	2
Total	99 =	46	42	11	Total	99 =	46	42	11

The table shows that the sample consists of firms taken from a cross section of industries. When a firm operates in more than one market the problem of assigning the firm to a particular industry arises. However, the problem was resolved by considering the main product of the firm that contributes maximum to its total revenue and assignment of the firm to a particular industry was made accordingly.

Any method of industrial classification suffers from certain inherent drawbacks and is subject to questioning of meaningfulness of such classifications. But in the absence of any better widely accepted approach, R.B.I. classification was accepted.

A study of the above table reveals that almost 89% of the sample firms belong to the first two groups. Moreover, the total number of firms belonging to 1st and 2nd group is almost equal. In the third group, there are minimum number of firms totalling 11 only and these companies may be treated as "deemed" government companies.

The performance of a firm is highly dependent on the type of industry to which it belongs. Industry wise classification of the sample firms shows, a good number of companies belong to cotton textile (11), Engineering (23), Chemicals (16). Studies depending on situation rely both on industry wise approach and pooled data approach from all industries.

As the number of companies belonging to the third group is minimum, there are a number of Industries where there is no firm belonging to this group, for example cotton textile. As a result, during the empirical studies, when within an industry intergroup comparison is made, it may be limited within two groups instead of three.

Apart from industry characteristics, size is an important determinant that influences the performance of a firm. All the sample firms were the member of 250 top companies of India ranked according to the assets, at least once during the period under study. Sizewise distribution of sample firms among the top 250 companies of India as on 1979 is shown in Table 2.2.

It shows all the firms under consideration are very big and have considerable influence upon the economy of the country. Moreover, they enjoy some privilege so far as size influences the performance of the corporation.

It would be further interesting and relevant to study the distribution of sample firms among big business houses who manage the firm on behalf of the institutions.

Table 2.2

Sizewise Distribution of Sample Firms

Rank based on total assets	*Number of companies*		*% of the total (approx.)*
1 - 50	28	companies	29%
51 - 100	15	"	15%
101 - 150	11	"	11%
151 - 200	15	"	15%
201 - 250	12	"	12%
above	18	"	18%
Total	99		100

Table 2.3

Housewise Distribution of Sample Firms

Name of the House	*Number*
1. Amin	1
2. A.C.C.	1
3. Ashokleyland	1
4. Bangur	9
5. Birla	9
6. F.C.C.	5
7. Kirloskar	4
8. Mafatlal	2
9. Mahindra	2
10. Parry	3
11. ShriRam	3
12. Singhania	3
13. Tata	11
14. Thapar	3
15. Raunaq	2
16. Lalbhai	2
17. I.C.I.	3
18. Others	35
Total	99

While the central purpose of the present study is to judge the efficiency of the management controlled firm, above classification will help in the process to judge the attitude of big business houses towards public money.

2.5 Time Period Studied

Most of the empirical analysis of the following chapters is confined to the sample firms over the period 1979-83. The choice of this particular period was dictated by the following considerations.

Firstly, the period may be considered as a "normal period" that has neither experienced unprecedented boom nor depression. Just after this period industry experienced a boom and the stock market share price index reached a record high.

Secondly, though not much important, this is the time period when the debate on the "role of institutions in the private corporate sector" once again came to the surface due to some controversial takeover attempts by N.R.I.

Five years time period from 1979-83 has been considered, which is sufficiently long and is helpful for avoiding a larger element of chance in utilizing any shorter time period. Values of the four basic variables during this time period were obtained by averaging method.

2.6 Conclusions

1. It is clear from the above discussions that four variables that have been used to measure the efficiency of management controlled firms are widely used. Further, use of these variables will help to understand the relevance of Robin Marris theory in the Indian context.

2. Industry average has been considered as standard and the performance of management controlled firm will be compared with this standard. Industry average is a broad based standard or it may be called the minimum

standard which management controlled firm is expected to achieve.

3. Firms where institutional holding is equal to or more than 25% have been identified as management controlled firms. For these firms ownership lies with the financial institutions but they are managed by individuals or group on behalf of financial institutions. The cut off rate is recognised by Securities Contracts Regulation Act.

   For an intergroup comparison within the management controlled firms two further cut off rates have also been considered.

4. Sample firms belong to a cross section of industry, they are very big in size and enjoy the benefit that is associated with size. Most of the firms belong to the first two groups. Industry-wise distribution shows almost half of the companies belong to cotton textile (11) engineering (23) and chemicals (16) industries.

5. In order to minimize the element of chance a longer time period of 5 years (1979-83) has been considered.

NOTES AND REFERENCES

1. For some of the examples see Radice HK, "Control Type, Profitability and Growth in Large Firms : An Empirical Study", The Economic Journal, September, 1971, pp. 547-562, Kania and McKean, "Ownership, Control and the Contemporary Corporation : A General Behaviour Analysis", Kyklos, Vol. 29, 1976, pp. 272-291.

2. R.L. Marris, The Economic Theory of Managerial Capitalism, London, 1964.

3. For a lucid discussion on the topic see P. Hall, "Effect of Control Type on the Performance of the Firms in the U.K.", Journal of Industrial Economics, 23, 1976, pp. 257-272.

4. Thonet and Poensgen, "Managerial Control and Economic Performance in West Germany", The Journal of Industrial Economics, September, 1979, pp. 23-25.

5. Growth as an objective of firm has been identified by Frank Knight, Joseph Schumpeter and Robert Gordon long before the explicit formulations of managerial theories. With these earlier authors, the pursuit of size was not restricted to the hired or professional managers. In fact Knight and Schumpeter discussed the tendency to build empires primarily in the context of owner entrepreneur. Schumpeter (The Theory of Economic Development, Harvard University Press, Cambridge, 1934, p. 93) recognised as the first drive of the entrepreneur" the dream and the will to found a kingdom". Knight (Risk, Uncertainty and Profit, Houghton Hifflin Company, Boston and New York 1921, p. 162) emphasized "the impulse to create" and impulse for which "increased income is not the dominant motive". Similarly Gordon (Business Leadership in the Large Corporation, University of California Press, Berkeley, 1961, pp. 331-332) noted that the tendency to continue to expand in the face of declining profit may be no stronger (among professional managers) than among many owner entrepreneurs whose devotion to their firms may lead them to continue to plough back earnings". Even Marris (The Economic Theory of 'Managerial' Capitalism, Macmillan, London, 1967, p. 10) concedes "there is nothing in the rules of traditional capitalism to require an owner manager to exclude all forms of satisfaction other than money".

6. This market is concerned with the buying and selling of voting stock and their effects on company control.

7. Peter Hall, "Control Type and the Market for Corporate Control in Large U.S. Corporations", The Journal of Industrial Economics, Vol. XXV June, 1977, p. 26.

8. J.E. Meade, 'Is "the New Industrial State" inevitable' Economic Journal, June 1968, p. 387.

9. Peter Hall, op. cit., 1977.

10. Punitive action denotes replacement of the existing Management. It represents discipline in its most extreme form.

11. There are a lot of writings on the particular issue, 'Executive Control Charts' prepared by E.I. du Pont de Nemours & Company Delaware, Wellington, 1960, very nicely shows the link between Variables that affect the performance of a firm.

12. For a discussion on the topic see Durand David "Cost of Debt and Equity Funds for Business : Trends and Problems of Measurement" reprinted in, The Management of Corporate Capital, Ezra Solomon (Ed.), New York, The Free Press, 1959, pp. 91-116, Brigham Eugene F. and Ramon E. Johnsons (Eds.), Issues in Managerial Finance, Hinsdale, Illinois, Dryden Press, 1976, p. 256. Modigliani and Miller, "The Cost of Capital, Corporation Finance and the Theory of Investment", American Economic Review, 43 (June 1958), pp. 261-297.

13. Thonet and Poensgen, op. cit., p. 24.

14. William McEachern, "Corporate Control and Growth : An Alternative Approach", The Journal of Industrial Economics, March 1978, p. 260.

15. Based on the above logic though the sample firms have been identified as management control, keeping in view thrust of the present study-to investigate economic implications of huge institutional holding on the performance of the firm, this controversial issue can temporarily be set aside. However, there is the scope of empirical testing whether the characteristics associated with management or owner controlled firms predominate in the sample firm. Exercise that has also been undertaken in the present study.

Comparison of the Characteristics of the Management Controlled Firm with Industry Average : Univariate Analysis

In the previous chapter an attempt was made to describe the variables used, to introduce the sample and to provide a definition of management controlled firm in the Indian context. Discussions of the following chapters now proceed directly to the main policy issue and related questions described in Chapter I, such as (I) What role financial institutions as a major shareholders play in the private corporate sector specially in the context of takeover? and (II) What are the specific goals that management control firm strives to achieve in exclusion of others?

To examine these questions purely from economic point of view, the following two chapters analyse the economic and financial characteristics of the management control firm and compare them with that of the industry average. Further within the sample, intergroup comparison has also been made to study the relationship between institution holding and performance of the firm. In the present chapter both parametric and non-parametric methods have been applied to test the two hypothesis. Section 3.1 to section 3.4 mainly depends upon parametric test and section 3.5 and 3.6 relies on non-parametric test statistics. Section 3.7 summarises the findings of this chapter.

3.1 Relative Characteristics of Management Controlled Firms and That of Others - A First Glance

It is proposed first to review in a very general way the nature of the differences which exist between the management controlled firms and that of others. Table 3.1 shows in simple, commonsense terms, without the use of any statistical test, how the economic characteristics of the management controlled firms differ from those of industry average. The table provides a first glance at the relative characteristics of the two groups of firms. With respect to any particular characteristics, say profitability, it simply shows how profitable the average management control firm is relative to the industry average. The table is presented here for purely illustrative purpose. The table has two parts, in one part industry wise analysis has been made and in other part analysis is based on pooled data across the industries.

Table 3.1

Relative Characteristics of the Firms (Having Institutional Holding Equal to or more than 25%) and that of Industry Average : A First Glance (1979-83)* Pooled Data

	Variable	*Industry mean*	*Mean of the sample*	*Mean of the sample firm as % of industry mean*
X1	Pretax profitability	6.99	5.91	84.55%
X2	Growth rate	14.75	13.58	92.07%
X3	Valuation ratio	1 (standard)	.705	70.5%
X4	Earnings to equity	13.10	12.57	95.94%

Relative Characteristics of Management Controlled Firms and that of Industry Average-Specific Industry Approach - A First Glance 1979-83

Table 3.1 (a) Cotton Textile (N = 11)

	Variable	*Industry mean*	*Mean of the sample*	*Mean of the sample firm as % of industry mean*
X1	Pretax Profitability	3.35	6.67	199.00%
X2	Growth rate	18.94	13.30	70.22%
X3	Valuation ratio	1	.73	73.00%
X4	Earnings to equity	11.23	12.77	113.7%

Table 3.1 (b) Engineering (N = 23)

	Variable	*Industry mean*	*Mean of the sample*	*Mean of the sample firm as % of industry mean*
X1	Pretax Profitability	7.90	6.64	84.00%
X2	Growth rate	21.09	17.86	84.68%
X3	Valuation ratio	1	.94	94.00%
X4	Earnings to equity	17.71	19.18	108.3%

Table 3.1 (c) Chemicals (N = 16)

	Variable	*Industry mean*	*Mean of the sample*	*Mean of the sample firm as % of industry mean*
X1	Pretax Profitability	8.33	7.41	88.9%
X2	Growth rate	23.76	10.21	42.97%
X3	Valuation ratio	1	.69	69.00%
X4	Earnings to equity	14.21	12.42	87.40%

* For each variable, the figure for the average management controlled firm is expressed as a percentage of that for the corresponding industry average.

Certain important points emerge from table 3.1. Firstly, performance of the management control firm in terms of four variables is always lower than that of industry average, though their magnitude varies from variable to variable. Say, in the case of profitability it is (84.5%) and valuation ratio (70.5%). Sample firm has a worst record in respect to other two variables also.

Secondly, specific industry wise analysis reveal a slightly different picture. For example, chemical industry almost shows the same trend with that of the calculation based on pooled data. Their performance in respect to all the four variables is lower than that of respective industry average. On the other hand, cotton textile industry has done fairly well at least in respect of two variables (profitability and earnings to equity). Pretax profitability of the sample firm is almost double than that of industry average. Whereas, growth and valuation ratio of the industry follows the trend of pooled data. For engineering, earnings to equity is the only variable that shows certain exceptional behaviour from the findings of pooled data. It will be unfair to make any serious comment on the basis of the above analysis. The table has been provided purely for the purpose of illustration and obviously it suffers from certain serious drawbacks. So no specific conclusion can be arrived at regarding the extent of differences between the average characteristics of the two groups of firms.

The above analysis can at best provide certain crude impression based on a general reading of the data regarding the differences that exist between two groups of firms. In order to arrive at more reliable conclusions about the nature of these differences, it is necessary to study the comparative group characteristics in much greater detail. In particular it is not enough and can in fact be quite misleading, to compare the two groups on the basis of their average characteristics. Proper analysis requires both a knowledge and a comparison of within group variation of these characteristics. In the same way, it is also necessary to study the degree of overlap between the groups with respect to various characteristics. Such questions, apart from their intrinsic interest are of course related to that of assessing the statistical significance of the observed differences in the above analysis.

The above mentioned problems are investigated in the next section.

3.2 Pooled Data, All Industries and Time Period : Univariate Analysis

Different statistical tests are used in this section on a univariate basis to compare the characteristics of two groups of firms. In the first stage all industries approach will be adopted, then specific industry wise analysis will be carried on.

(a) Test of Differences of Mean

It is hypothesised that there is no difference in the mean value of the characteristics of two groups of firm i.e. management controlled and others. On the basis of the assumption, result of the statistical test is shown in table 3.2 & 3.2 (a).

Table 3.2

Comparison of the characteristics of Management Controlled Firms with Industry Average (1979-83)

(Pooled Data, All Industries and Time Period)

Variable	*Industry mean*	*Sample mean of 99 companies*	*S.D. of mean of sample firm*	*Difference of mean*	*No. of companies below industry average*	*No. of companies above industry average*	*Total*
X1 Pretax Profitability	6.99	5.91	5.88	-1.08(b)	66	33	99
X2 Growth rate	14.75	13.58	9.78	-1.17	70	29	99
X3 Valuation ratio	1	.705	1.51	-.295(b)	62	22	84
X4 Earnings to equity	13.10	12.57	14.52	-.53	50	41	91

Table 3.2 (a)

Groupwise Classification of Sample Firm : Comparison of Their Records with Industry Average (1979-83)

Group-I (Institutional holding ≥ 25% but < 33 1/3%, N = 46

	Variable	*Industry mean*	*Sample*	*S.D. of mean of sample firm*	*Difference of mean*	*No. of companies below industry average*	*No. of companies above industry average*	*Total*
X1	Pretax Profitability	6.99	4.65	5.57	-2.34[a]	33	13	46
X2	Growth rate	14.75	12.08	1.32	-2.67[c]	35	11	46
X3	Valuation ratio	1	.71	.98	-.29[b]	25	12	37
X4	Earnings to equity	13.10	9.89	17.48	-3.21	27	18	45

Group II (Institutional holding ≥33 1/3% but < 50%) N = 42

X1	Pretax Profitability	6.99	6.02	5.58	-.97	28	14	42
X2	Growth rate	14.75	14.88	8.64	.13	26	16	42
X3	Valuation ratio	1	.75	1.34	-.25[c]	29	8	37
X4	Earnings to equity	13.10	13.39	11.13	.29	18	19	37

Group III (Institutional holding ≥ 50%) N = 11

X1	Pretax Profitability	6.99	10.18	6.67	3.19[c]	5	6	11
X2	Growth rate	14.75	10.66	8.69	-4.09[c]	9	2	11
X3	Valuation ratio	1	.6	2.69	-.4[a]	8	2	10
X4	Earnings to equity	13.10	15.48	8.24	2.38	5	4	9

(a) Significance at 1%

(b) Significance at 5%

(c) Significance at 10% level.

While preparing the tables all industry approach has been adopted. The first part of the table 3.2 compares the characteristics of all sample firms with industry average. The other part of the table 3.2 (a) divides the sample firm into three groups and compares the performance of each group with industry average. The purpose of grouping the firms is to compare the performance of each group separately and to have a first hand idea regarding the impact of increase in institutional holding on the performance of the management controlled firm.

Although the figures in table 3.2 and 3.2 (a) are self explanatory, nevertheless, since these tables contain a large amount of information a brief description of some of them will be in order. Turning to table 3.2, it clearly indicates the performance of management controlled firm in respect of all the four variables is worse than that of industry average. For two variables, profitability and valuation ratio, difference is statistically significant at 5% level. Columns 6 and 7 show a large number of firms failed to achieve the standard. However, before drawing any implications from this proportion further statistical analysis is required in this respect. At least, it provides a crude trend regarding the proportion of firms failing to achieve the standard.

Perhaps, it will not be out of context to mention here that the four variables - profitability, growth, valuation and earnings to equity are interrelated with one another. Though, their relationship is not that much straightforward, it can reasonably be assumed that a decline in profitability of the firm would have certain adverse affect on the market value of the share, causing a decline in the valuation ratio.

Quite naturally tables 3.1 and 3.2 show the same trend regarding the performance of management controlled firms. Results obtained from table 3.2 are more significant than that of table 3.1, in the sense, it helps to identify the variables that can statistically discriminate between the two groups of firms. Hence, the findings of table 3.2 are more reliable and reduce the possibility of misclassification.

Table 3.2 (a) shows, among three groups, performance of the first group, that consists of the maximum number of firms nearly 50% of the total sample, is the worst. The group failed to achieve standard in respect of all the four variables. In respect of the three variables - profitability, growth and valuation ratio there are statistically significant differences between this group and that of others.

A comparison of the performance of three groups at the first instance, may provide an impression, that the performance of the management controlled firm improves as the holding of institution increases. For example, in the case of the third group where institutional holding is maximum, at least for two variables - profitability and return on equity, their performance is better than that of industry average. It may further be noted that while profitability of this group is significantly higher than that of others, the other variable i.e. growth is substantially lower. One of the probable reason of it, considering present capital market condition, in order to foster growth rate of company, the company has to depend upon financial institution. Where the holding of financial institution has already reached to a critical level of 50% for the companies of this group, the manager of the corporation may decide to sacrifice growth rate to reduce dependence on the institution.

A comparison of group I and group II that also consists of a large number of firms will provide the same impression that the performance of management controlled firms improves with the increase in institutional holding. Obviously, this type of intergroup comparison is very crude and there is further scope of using sophisticated technique to arrive at the right conclusion.

Though the analysis of this section is much more useful and reliable in comparison with the analysis carried on in section 3.1, it also suffers from the following drawbacks hence to be accepted with reservation.

(1) The analysis suffers from statistical bias that may arise due to pooling of data. This issue that has been

treated elaborately in the next section.

(2) There is further scope of using appropriate statistical technique so as to facilitate meaningful intergroup comparison within a management controlled firm.

3.3 Statistical Analysis : The Problem of Pooling

In making statistical comparison of the characteristics of management controlled firms and that of others on a cross section basis, the first problem which arises is that of "Pooling". Is it desirable to compare the characteristics of two groups of firms within each year and each industry separately? Or is it desirable to pool firms across all the industries and all years? These are the two vital issues to be resolved before proceeding any further.

Pooling is obviously helpful from a statistical point of view in that it leads to larger samples and therefore to more reliable results. It is specially relevant for the present sample. Any broader classification of firms such as Agriculture and Allied Products, Processing and Manufacturing of Food Stuff will be very gross and misleading. Further, a detailed industry wise classification, though not completely free from criticism, is more scientific. If a detailed classification is followed, the number of firms belonging to each industry group will be minimum for any meaningful statistical analysis. So considering number of sample firms, it would be better to pool the firms across all the industries or sample design to be changed.

Secondly, any analysis based on detailed industry classification requires each firm to be assigned to a particular industry group to which it belongs. The problem with this approach is, most of the big business now a days are well diversified and do not fit neatly within any particular industry group. Hence, any such attempt would be to some extent arbitrary. Pooling firms across industries would be free from this problem.

Obviously there are also certain problems of pooling

firms across the industries. One of the basic factor affecting firm performance is the structure of the industry in which a firm is located. Industry characteristics include degree of competition, growth opportunity, barriers to entry etc. Since all industries will differ in structure to some extent, it would be difficult to isolate the effect of control type if firms are compared across industry lines. For example, previous researchers have assumed that firms within the same industry have similar investment opportunities. If the sample firms within a particular industry achieve a growth rate which is lower than the industry average, then it may be concluded that considering the peculiar industry characteristics, management controlled firms fail to achieve targeted growth rate and vice versa.

Secondly, legitimacy of pooling depends upon the characteristics of the firms being pooled. If there are major differences in the characteristics of the firms among the samples which are being pooled, this introduces an important source of bias in the analysis. It is easy to construct numerical examples to show that on account of this bias it may be concluded from statistical analysis that there is no difference between management controlled firms and others when in fact they exist and vice versa.

It is, therefore, relevant to find out how legitimate pooling over the industries is from this particular point of view. For this purpose, the mean profitability of all companies within each industry for each year as reported in R.B.I. bulletin may be compared. As an illustration of the results, and for their own interest, a selection from these calculations, relating to one individual characteristics of company records in two industries, is presented in table 3.3.

Average pretax profitability of firms within chemical industry is much higher than cotton textile industry and often it is several times than that of cotton textiles. Due to this inter-industry differences, pooling data across industries could, therefore, produce results which are seriously biased, unless a suitable sample design is used to overcome this problem.

Table 3.3

Pretax Profitability : Cotton Textile and Chemicals 1979-83

Year	*Cotton Textile mean R.O.I. %*	*Chemicals mean R.O.I. %*
79	6.9%	13.9%
80	8.3%	12.9%
81	17.5%	9.7%
82	1.00%	6.4%
83	1.00%	5.6%

Lastly, particular industry characteristics may also influence the objective, management of the corporation will strive for. Suppose, in an industry where there is no scope of growth, obviously management of the corporation will try for other goal than growth. Otherwise uneconomic growth will lower the earnings of shareholders and thereby market value of shares and the company may be subject to takeover bid.

Considering the pros and cons of both the methods, it may be concluded that the results obtained from particular industry approach would be more reliable as it takes into cognizance the inter industry differences. The approach that has been adopted in many earlier studies and has also been followed in the next sectionl. Due to paucity of sufficient number of firms within each industry group to permit any meaningful statistical analysis, only three industries such as cotton textile (11), Engineering (23) and Chemicals (16) have been considered for further investigation in section 3.4.

3.4 Test of Differences - Specific Industry Approach

One way to overcome bias that may arise due to pooling to adopt the specific industry approach, where performance of sample firm belonging to each industry is measured separately and is compared with their respective industry record. Adopting this approach, results of three industries such as engineering, textile and chemical are given.

Table 3.4

Test of Differences of Mean-Specific Industry Approach (a statement of comparative characteristics of firm 1979-83)

General Engineering (Institutional Holding ≥ 25% N = 23

Variable	Industry mean	Sample	S.D. of mean of sample firm	Difference of mean	No. of companies below	No. of companies above industry average	Total
X1 Pretax Profitability	7.90	6.64	3.86	-1.26[c]	17	6	23
X2 Growth rate	21.09	17.84	4.64	-3.25[a]	18	5	23
X3 Valuation ratio	1	.94	.27	-.06	17	6	23
X4 Earning to equity	17.71	19.18	10.61	1.47	14	9	23

Cotton Textile (Institutional Holding ≥ 25%) N = 11

Variable	Industry mean	Sample	S.D. of mean of sample firm	Difference of mean	No. of companies below	No. of companies above industry average	Total
X1 Pretax Profitability	3.35	6.67	4.71	3.32[b]	4	7	11
X2 Growth rate	18.94	13.30	2.95	-5.64[a]	10	1	11
X3 Valuation ratio	1	.73	.20	-.27[a]	10	1	11
X4 Earning to equity	11.23	12.77	8.67	1.54	7	3	10

Chemicals (Institutional holding ⩾ 25%) N = 16

	Variable	Industry mean	Sample	S.D. of mean of sample firm	Difference of mean	No. of companies below	above industry average	Total
X1	Pretax Profitability	8.33	7.41	4.35	- .92	11	5	16
X2	Growth rate	23.76	10.21	8.72	-13.55[a]	14	2	16
X3	Valuation ratio	1	.69	3.48	-.31	7	5	12
X4	Earnings to Equity	14.21	12.42	8.68	-1.79	8	4	12

1) (a) significant at 1%,
   (b) significant at 5%,
   (c) significant at 10% level.
2) all variables are expressed as %.
3) full information for all the companies are not available.

Information provided by table 3.4 is more reliable. The probability of misclassification between management controlled firm and others is also minimum.

A careful study of the above table will reveal that there is at least one variable e.g. growth rate, common to three industry groups that can discriminate the management controlled firms with that of others. For all the industry groups difference is significant at 1% level. There are different possible explanations of this particular phenomenon. Firstly, there is a line of thinking that the small firms find it easier to make big percentage increases than large units. Firms under consideration are all very big and belong to the top 250 companies of India, so there is little scope for these firms to grow any further. Secondly, the decision not to grow any further may be deliberate also, considering the size of the firms, it may be argued that these firms have an overall control over the market. They may decide to arrest the growth rate in such a way that will help for the maximum exploitation of the market in order to reap high profit. Thirdly, as the firms are very big, they come under direct control of M.R.T.P. Act, that may be instrumental for the slow growth rate of these companies. Whatever might be the reason, the fact remains that the growth rate of management controlled firm is lower than that of others and it is a good discriminator between these two groups of firms.

Valuation is another variable common to three industry groups where sample firm failed to achieve the standard. The difference is statistically significant at 1% level only in the case of cotton textile industry. It may be noted that the performance of textile industry considering two variables profitability and earnings to equity is quite satisfactory. Further, these are the two variables that influence the market price of shares heavily. It appears that there exists an inverse relationship between earnings and market price of share of sample firm. It is an interesting issue that requires further investigations but which is beyond the scope of the present study.

Earnings to equity, however, shows a different trend. Out of three sets of data, excepting chemical, performance of management controlled firm is better than that of industry average. The difference is never statistically significant at 10% or better level.

Profitability is also another good discriminator between these two groups of firms. Out of three sets of profit data in the above tables, only in the case of cotton textile, the performance of management controlled firm is better than other group. The difference is significant at 5% level. While in the case of engineering and chemical, management controlled firms failed to achieve the standard. Difference in the performance of engineering with that of industry average is also statistically significant at 10% level.

One must be careful while interpreting this result. The relationship between size and profitability is an extensively researched issue in the area of economics. There is a well known thesis that size and profitability is positively correlated. Applying this logic, it may be argued, the sample firms that are very big in size would show a better result on account of profitability than that of industry average. While industry average calculated on the basis of firms belonging to large and medium size industry.

Further a comparison of table 3.2 and 3.4 reveals that under specific industry approach, the number of variables that can discriminate between these two groups of firms increases. Specially in the case of cotton textile, three variables out of four are good discriminator among these two groups. It shows, if industry characteristics are properly incorporated in the analysis, it may provide a significantly different picture from all industry approach.

Groupwise analysis within each industry is shown in table 3.4 (a). It may be recalled, as the number of firms belonging to each group is minimum, there is scope of bias in the analysis. Further there are insignificant number of firms belonging to the third group for these industries and they have been totally avoided for the purpose of the analysis of this section. Accepting all these deficiencies of this section, it is believed that the analysis of this section will provide some idea, as to how the performance of the firms varies with the change in institutional holding within each industry.

3.4(a) Groupwise Classification of Firms within Each Industry : Comparison of Their Performance with Respective Industry Average

Table 3.4 (a)

General Engineering

(Institutional holding ≥ 25% but < 33 1/3%)

Group I, n = 11

Variable		*Industry mean*	*Sample*	*S.D. of sample mean*	*Difference of mean*	*No. of companies* below-above industry average		*Total*
X1	Pretax Profitability	7.9	5	3.44	-2.9[a]	9	2	11
X2	Growth rate	21.09	19.64	10.6	-1.45	8	3	11
X3	Valuation	1	.98	.24	-.02	9	2	11
X4	Earnings to equity	17.71	17.15	12.53	-.56	8	3	11

Group II, n = 9

(Institutional holding ≥ 33 1/3% but < 50%)

Variable		*Industry mean*	*Sample*	*S.D. of sample mean*	*Difference of mean*	*No. of companies* below-above industry average		*Total*
X1	Pretax Profitability	7.9	6.83	2.7	-1.07	6	3	9
X2	Growth rate	21.09	17.84	6.37	-3.25[c]	7	2	9
X3	Valuation	1	.92	.27	-.08	6	3	9
X4	Earning to equity	17.71	20.22	8.86	2.51	4	5	9

Table 3.4(a)

Chemicals

(Institutional holding ≥ 25% but < 33 1/3%)
Group I, n = 7

Variable		Industry mean	Sample	S.D. of sample mean	Difference of mean	No. of companies below-above industry average		Total
X1	Pretax profitability	8.33	5.57	5.26	-2.76	6	1	7
X2	Growth rate	23.76	10.34	5.55	-13.42[a]	7	0	7
X3	Valuation ratio	1	.58	.55	-.42	3	2	5

Group II, n = 5

(Institutional holding ≥ 33 1/3% but < 50%)

Variable		Industry mean	Sample	S.D. of sample mean	Difference of mean	No. of companies below-above industry average		Total
X1	Pretax profitability	8.33	7.37	2.97	-.96	4	2	6
X2	Growth rate	23.76	11.79	9.36	-11.97[b]	5	1	6
X3	Valuation ratio	1	1.07	4.23	.07	1	3	4

In view of very poor significance level of the statistics relating to Earning to Equity it has been omitted.

Table 3.4 (a)

Cotton Textile

(Institutional holding ⩾ 25% but < 33 1/3%)
Group I, n = 6

Variable	*Industry mean*	*Sample*	*S.D. of sample mean*	*Difference of mean*	*No. of companies* below-above industry average		*Total*
X1 Pretax profitability	3.35	5.91	3.46	2.56[c]	2	4	6
X2 Growth rate	18.94	8.26	2.74	-10.68[a]	6	0	6
X3 Valuation ratio	1	.74	.24	-.26[b]	5	1	6
X4 Earnings to equity	11.23	15.19	7.86	3.96	1	4	5

Group II (N = 5)
(Institutional holding ⩾ 33 1/3% but < 50%)

Variable	*Industry mean*	*Sample*	*S.D. of sample mean*	*Difference of mean*	*No. of companies* below-above industry average		*Total*
X1 Pretax profitability	3.35	7.01	5.75	3.66	2	3	5
X2 Growth rate	18.94	15.57	12.17	-3.37	4	1	5
X3 Valuation ratio	1	.69	.09	-.31[a]5	5	0	
X4 Earnings to equity	11.25	11.8	9.41	.55	2	3	5

(a) Significant at 1%
(b) at 5%
(c) at 10% level
All information for sample firm are not available.

Any attempt to interpret the tables in terms of change in the behaviour of management controlled firms with rise in institutional holding, based on simple observation of above data, may be very crude and unscientific. The approach which has been followed earlier while interpreting table 3.2 (a). The tables at best provide the necessary information as to how the performance of each group within a particular industry deviates from the standard. It fails to make any meaningful intergroup comparison.

So as to facilitate intergroup comparison, a simple statistical analysis, commonly known as "Distance Analysis" has been performed in section 3.4 (b) based on the data of tables in 3.4 (a). The analysis will help to identify the variables that can discriminate between different groups within management controlled firms of each industry.

3.4(b) Distance Analysis

Mahalanobis "Standardized Distance" model has been used to measure the distance between different groups within an industry. Differences between different groups can also be studied through mean differences. Mean difference between groups alongwith distance analysis will provide the scope of more meaningful and accurate analysis.

The whole issue may be put in the following way. Suppose there are some variables whose mean value significantly differs among two groups of a particular industry. The question now arises : what is the extent of discrimination achieved by these 'significant' variables? or to put it in another way, what is the degree of overlap between the groups with respect to these variables? Distance model would provide an idea regarding the proportion of firms misclassified and could serve as an index of the degree of overlap between them.

Mahalanobis distance between two groups is defined as being equal to d/s, where d is the difference between mean of two groups and s is an estimate of their common standard deviation. If the variable is normally distributed and has equal variance in both groups and the two populations are of the same size, there is a simple relationship between d/s and the probability of misclassification. Some values of this probability of given values of | d/s | are given below :-

d/s	Probability of misclassification %
0.000	50
0.251	45
0.501	40
0.771	35
1.049	30
1.349	25
1.683	20
2.073	15
2.563	10
3.290	5
4.653	1

Adopted from Ajit Singh "Take overs" Cambridge University Press, 1971, p. 69.

These figures show that when | d/s | = 0 i.e., when the two groups are literally indistinguishable, the probability of misclassification is at its maximum of 50%. In general, the greater the value of | d/s | the lower is the probability of misclassification and vice-versa. Although strictly speaking the relationship between | d/s | and the probability of misclassification holds only under the condition mentioned above, the statistics | d/s | can nevertheless be used as a rough index of the degree of overlap for most of the variables of the present study.[1]

Table 3.4 (b) shows mean differences and distance between two groups classified according to institutional holding for three industries under consideration.

Table 3.4 (b)

Mean Differences and Distance Between Groups - An Intergroup Comparison

Cotton Textile

Variable	*Group I*			*Group II*			*Comparison*		
	Mean	*S.D.*	*N*	*Mean*	*S.D.*	*N*	*Differences in mean*	*t*	*| d/s |*
Pretax profitability (X1)	5.91	3.46	6	7.01	5.75	5	-1.1	-.40	.24
Growth X2	8.26	2.74	6	15.57	12.17	5	-7.31	-1.46	.98
Valuation X3	.74	.24	6	.69	.09	5	.05	.45	.30
Earnings to equity X4	15.19	7.86	6	11.8	9.41	5	3.39	.66	.39

General Engineering

Variable	*Group I*			*Group II*			*Comparison*		
	Mean	*S.D.*	*N*	*Mean*	*S.D.*	*N*	*Differences in mean*	*t*	*| d/s |*
Pretax profitability (X1)	5.0	3.44	11	6.83	2.72	9	-1.83	-1.33	.60
Growth X2	19.64	10.6	11	17.84	6.37	9	1.8	.46	.21
Valuation X3	.98	.24	11	.92	.27	9	.06	.54	.24
Earnings to equity X4	17.15	12.53	11	20.22	8.86	9	-3.07	-.63	.29

Chemicals

Variable	*Group I*			*Group II*			*Comparison*		
	Mean	*S.D.*	*N*	*Mean*	*S.D.*	*N*	*Differences in mean*	*t*	*| d/s |*
Pretax profitability (X1)	5.57	5.26	7	7.37	2.97	6	-1.8	-.76	.44
Growth X2	10.34	5.55	7	11.79	9.36	6	-1.45	-.58	.19
Valuation X3	.58	.55	5	1.07	4.23	4	-.49	.26	.20

Table 3.4 (b) clearly shows, for all the industries, neither the mean differences nor the distance among two groups is significant. Almost all the variables have value of | d/s | of less than .5 (excepting XI for general engineering and X2 for cotton textile) indicating 40-45% chance of misclassification. The general conclusion that can be arrived at is that there is no statistical differences between different groups within an industry. The issue may also be stated in the following way- there is no evidence that the behaviour of management controlled firm changes with change in institutional holding. Although there is clear evidence that the performance of management controlled firm as a whole is worse than that of industry average for a number of variables.

Another way of testing the hypothesis under consideration is the use of non-parametric test. Findings of parametric and non-parametric test may be considered together to reach any conclusion regarding the hypothesis.

3.5 The Binomial Probability Test

Another method by which the characteristics of two groups of firms may be compared involves posing the problem in the following way. Suppose, there is little difference between management controlled firms and others for each variable. Then it can be expected that there is .5% chance for each management controlled firm within an industry meeting the average. Obviously, the logical consequence is, there is another .5% chance for each industry and each variable not meeting the standard. So it can be hypothesised - there is no differences in the characteristics of management controlled firms and others. By counting the actual number of management controlled firms that failed to attain the industry average in respect of each variable, the hypothesis of no difference can be tested easily.

Such a test not only has an obvious intuitive appeal, but also possesses the advantage of being distribution free. Further binomial probability test is one of the simplest way to avoid the difficulties that may arise due to pooling. Hence, pooled data can be used, without any serious statistical bias that may arise out of it. The process involves a comparison of the records of each management controlled firms with the average record of firms in the same industry for the same period. For this particular test, pooling does not lead to any obvious statistical bias. The results of the test, for the data pooled across all industries and time periods are given in table 3.5. The table also includes the test of pooling data across chemical, cotton textile and engineering industry - three industries that have been emphasized in the present study. Further to facilitate comparison with mean difference study, test has also been applied to these three industries separately.[2]

Table 3.5

Comparison of the Records of Management Controlled Firms with Respective Industry Average : Pooled Data, all Industries and Time Period, Binomial Probability Test

Variable	*Number of firm*	*% < industry average*
Pretax profitability (X1)	88	57.9
Growth (X2)	88	77.3[(a)]
Valuation (X3)	84	73.8[(a)]
Earnings to equity (X4)	88	53.0

3.5(a) Pooled Data for Chemical, Engineering and Cotton Textile - Comparison of Records of Management Controlled Firm with Respective Industry Average : Binomial Probability Test

Table 3.5 (a)

Variable	*Number of firm*	*% < industry average*
Pretax Profitability (X1)	50	64.0
Growth (X2)	50	84.0[(a)]
Valuation (X3)	46	73.9[(a)]
Earnings to equity (X4)	45	55.0

Table 3.5 (b)

Comparison of Records of Management Controlled Firm with Respective Industry Average - Binomial Probability Test

Variable	*Chemical*		*Cotton Textile*		*Engineering*	
	No. of firm	*% < industry average*	*No. of firm*	*% < industry average*	*No. of firm*	*% < industry average*
Pretax profitability (X1)	16	68.7[c]	11	36.4	23	73.9[b]
Growth (X2)	16	87.5[a]	11	90.9[a]	23	78.2[a]
Valuation (X3)	12	58.3	11	91 [a]	23	73.9[b]
Earnings to equity (X4)	12	66.7	10	30.0	23	60.9

(a) = significant at 1% level.
(b) = significant at 5% level.
(c) = significant at 10% level.

All the tables under subsection 3.5 show that there are significant differences between the two groups of firms for several variables. In many a cases findings contradict the hypothesis of no difference. The over all picture which emerges from the above analysis is that the management controlled firm has a worse record than the average industry performance. For example, in the case of pooled data for all industries the percentage of firms failed to achieve respective industry average are 57.9% for XI, 77.3% for X2, 73.8% for X3 and 53% for X4. A look at the other tables will also reveal the same picture.

When the same hypothesis has been tested by applying two different statistical techniques, it becomes necessary to make a comparative analysis among them. It would be fruitless to make a comparison between the results obtained by binomial probability test for all industries with that of the test of mean differences for all industries in table 3.2. The primary reason is, different methodology has been adopted in two cases to compare the performance of management controlled firms. This type of comparison will be helpful if the results obtained by binomial probability test for chemical, textile and engineering are compared with mean difference analysis for the same industries in table 3.4. A study of these two tables reveals a close similarity in results under these two approaches. Almost the same set of variables under these two methods can discriminate between management controlled firms and others.

Another interesting feature that emerges from the above tables is that growth (X2) is the variable where a large number of management controlled firms fail to achieve the target of respective industry average. The percentage of firms failing to achieve respective industry average are 77.3% for all industries, 84% for engineering, chemical, textile industries combined, 87.5% for chemical, 90.9% for cotton textile, and 78.2% for engineering. On all the occasions the difference is statistically significant at 1% level. This trend was also apparent in the case of mean difference analysis in section 3.2 and 3.4. The probable explanation of which has already been provided in those sections.

No further analysis of the above table is necessary. The reason is both parametric and non-parametric tests provide almost the same result, specially when the same sample design has been followed. As a result, most of the explanations have already been provided earlier. The issue that is emphasised is the similarity of findings under these two different approaches.

3.6 Kruskal-Wallis Test

From the above discussions it is evident that there are a number of variables which can discriminate between management controlled firms and others. This section is an attempt to make an intergroup comparison among management controlled firms on the basis of non-parametric test statistics. First part of the analysis considers pooled data across all the industries and tries to show whether there is any statistical differences between three groups of management controlled firms. The second part adopts specific industry approach, considers two groups of firms instead of three within each industry and attempts to make a comparison among them.

Different statistical techniques are widely used to test the significance of the difference between more than two sample means. The most popular method is ANOVA. For the purpose of the present section non-parametric test has been used based on Kruskal-Wallis model. The test is considered relevant on two accounts. First, the assumption of normality with equal variances underlying F test in one-way ANOVA may not hold good. Second, Kruskal-Wallis test is not as sensitive to the assumption of equal variances as in ANOVA. Third, it is free from any assumption regarding distribution.

The data are measured under non-parametric test only by scores on an ordinal scale, hence, the only appropriate descriptor of change in efficiency in any group is the median score. So, the null hypothesis to be tested is that the median scores are equal for the three groups, with M1 denoting the median of the ith group. Hypothesis set can be written as -

$$H : M_1 = M_2 = M_3$$

To test the null hypothesis of equality of population mean across the three groups of firm characterized by institutional holding, Kruskal-Wallis test was performed on rank transformed data for the respective variable. The results are given in table 3.6.

Table 3.6

Results of Kruskal Wallis Test
Pooled Data for all Industries and Time
Period Classified into Three Groups

Variable	*N*	*Test statistics (H)*
Pretax Profitability (X1)	99	4.829[a]
Growth (X2)	84	2.551
Valuation (X3)	91	0.813
Earnings to equity (X4)	91	0.925

(1) a.p. < .10

(2) P value corresponding to test statistics H has been determined assuming asymptotic sampling distribution of H. This approximate asymptotic P value is then found as a right tail probability from the chi-square table with (K-1) degrees of freedom, K being the number of groups.

(3) All the test statistics have been adjusted for tied observations.

The table shows at least in the case of profitability null hypothesis of equality of mean is rejected. It implies that there is a difference between three groups at least for variable X_1. However, in order to answer which pairs of groups differ significantly from each other, a technique known as multiple comparison is to be applied.[3] For this purpose Dunn's procedure of multiple comparison has been adopted.

Table 3.6 (a)

Results of Multiple Comparison with Respect to Profitability

	Group Ri	*Group i*		
		1	*2*	*3*
		$\mid \bar{R}i\text{-}55.67 \mid$	$\mid \bar{R}i\text{-}47.53 \mid$	$\mid \bar{R}i\text{-}35.68 \mid$
1.	55.67	0		
2.	47.53	8.14	0	
3.	35.68	19.99[a]	11.85	0

$\bar{R}i$ = Ri/ni denotes the mean of the ranks corresponding to i th group of n i observations.

a = significant at 15% level.

From the above two tables conclusions that can be drawn are 1) Profitability is the only variable that can discriminate between three groups of management controlled firm. 2) It further shows that as the institutional holding increases profitability tends to decrease. One of the possible explanation of this type of behaviour is, as the institutional holding increases, investment of "manager" of the business decreases and they become reluctant so far as the proper use of public money is concerned causing decline in the profitability of the firm.

It may be argued, though the analysis of intergroup comparison comes within the objective of the study outlined in chapter I, it has got little relevance in the perspective of broad policy issue of the present study. Once the firms have been identified as management controlled, it is their economic performance as a group that matters so it is immaterial how the performance within group changes.

However, this type of analysis would be helpful to provide answers to the questions such as - does the managerial exploitation of owner increases with rise in institutional holdings within the management control firm? Does it effect the growth policy of the firm? etc. An interesting information is available from the above analysis. Firms that belong to the third group, where institutional holding equal to or more than 50%, has a worst record in terms of profitability. Legally, these companies may be described as government companies. Further, if their performance record is considered, it might be an useful information to decide upon the role of institutions in these companies.

However, specific industry approach to discriminate among different groups of management controlled firm would be more appropriate and permit to make a comparative study with the parametric test of section 3.4 (b). At this stage also two groups within the management controlled firms belonging to each industry have been considered. To compare the performance of two groups, appropriate non-parametric test statistics is Mann-Whitney U Test instead of Kruskal-Wallis test that has been applied in the next section.

3.6(b) Mann-Whitney U Test

Like Kruskal-Wallis test, Mann-Whitney test is also performed on the basis of ranking of data. The test enables to determine whether two independent samples have been drawn from the same population. Hypothesis can be stated in the following way -

$$H_o = R_{(Xi)} = R_{(Yi)}$$

Null hypothesis is average of the rank of Groups X and Y, which is approximately equal. The results of the Mann-Whitney U test for three industries are given below -

Table 3.6 (b)

Results of Mann-Whitney U Test - An Intergroup Comparison for Three Industries

Variables	Textile		General Engineering		Chemical	
	ΣR_{xi}	T	ΣR_{xi}	T	ΣR_{xi}	T
Pretax profitability (X1)	39	18	96	30 [b]	41	13
Growth (X2)	34	13	103	37	47	19
Valuation (X3)	33.5	12.5	97	31 [c]	14	4
Earnings to equity (X4)	19	9	105	39	33	18

(b) significant at 5% level.
(c) significant at 10% level.

The above table clearly shows, excepting for two variables in the general engineering, two groups belonging to each industry are indistinguishable. The findings have a close similarity with the distance analysis of section 3.4 (b). Practically, test of mean differences, distance analysis and non-parametric test provides the same result that there is no difference between different groups within management controlled firm.

It is to be mentioned here, that the non-parametric test that has been used in this section is not free from criticism. Specially non-parametric test is not that much efficient or "sharp" as parametric test. A lot of information is ignored in non-parametric test thus reducing its credibility. However, if the findings of both parametric and non-parametric tests are considered simultaneously it may provide better guide-lines regarding the hypothesis under consideration.

3.6 Conclusions

Empirical studies of the present chapter mainly deal with two issues -

(a) Considering certain major economic and financial variables whether it is possible to discriminate between management controlled firms and others,

(b) Considering the same economic variables, is it possible to make any distinction between different groups within the management controlled firm?

These two questions are directly related with the main policy issue of the present study - the role of financial institutions in the private corporate sector, specially in the context of take over.

So far as the first issue is concerned, empirical studies of the present chapter provides a quite reasonable evidence that the performance of management controlled firm for a number of variables is worse than that of industry average. It may be recalled, the firms that have been selected for the purpose of the present study are virtually government owned firms. The firms are managed by individual or group on behalf of the government. It is evident that managers failed to manage the resources entrusted to them economically.

So far the second issue is concerned, in the first part of the study, certain conclusions were drawn simply on the basis of general reading of data. In most cases, group performance was compared with industry average and sometimes certain crude conclusions were drawn simply by comparing the results of different variables of different groups. Only in the last part of the study specially from section 3.4, serious attempt has been made to differentiate the performance among different groups within the management controlled firms. Overall conclusion that can be arrived is, there is practically no statistical differences among different groups within the management controlled firms.

However, it is felt that there is the necessity to study

rigorously the relationship between institutional holding and efficiency of the firm measured in terms of the variables under consideration. The issues that are to be examined in this context are - what are the variables apart from control type that effect performance of the firm? How much separation of ownership from control is responsible for the inefficient functioning of the management control firm? Whether owner controlled firms were better managed than management controlled firms?

A thorough investigation of all these issues would be helpful for an understanding of the reasons of inefficient functioning of institution owned firms.

NOTES AND REFERENCES

1. If the underlying populations are not equal in size, as indeed they are not in the present case, the statistics | d/s | can however still be used as a measure of the degree of overlap between the groups. For a detailed discussions and application see Ajit Singh, Takeover, Cambridge, 1971, pp. 68-69.

2. Strictly speaking, in order for the binomial probability test to be completely non-parametric, the median rather than the (unweighted) arithmetic mean should be used as a measure of the 'average'. Since the mean values were readily available and calculation of the medians for such a large number of sets of data would have been a laborious task, mean value has been used for this exercise. For an application of this approach see Ajit Singh, op. cit., p. 66.

3. For a description of the test see Jean Dickinson Gibbon, Non Parametric Tests for Quantitative Analysis, Holt, Rinehart and Winston, 1976, pp. 175-183.

CHAPTER FOUR

Control Criteria - Its Impact on the Performance of Firms - Multivariate Analysis

Introduction

In the last chapter an attempt was made to discriminate on the basis of four economic criteria between management controlled firms and others on a univariate basis. A comparison of the records of the two groups of firms reveals that there are significant differences between the two groups for several of the four basic variables considered in the study. However, a comparison of the characteristics of the different groups within the management controlled firm showed that they are practically indistinguishable.

There is a shift in the attention in the present chapter in two directions. Firstly, the present chapter relies on multivariate analysis for further investigation of issue under consideration, instead of univariate analysis followed in the last chapter. Secondly, an attempt is made in this section to discriminate between the records of management controlled firms and owner controlled firms in lieu of industry average as followed in the last chapter. This departure in attention is made for the following reasons.

The purpose of the statistical analysis of the present

section is to investigate to what extent, if at all, control type affects the performance of firms. In the background of the analysis of the earlier chapter, the scope may also be restated in the following way. To what extent, if at all, inefficiency of the management controlled firms is attributable for separation of ownership from control (control type). It is accepted, apart from nature of control that there are different variables that might also influence the performance of the firms. So there is the necessity to develop a statistical technique capable of distinguishing the effects of these variables so that influences of control type (owner or manager) can be identified properly. This will be helpful for a better understanding of the effect of nature of control on the inefficient functioning of the management controlled firms under study. Application of multivariate analysis is a right step in this direction and findings based on a much more sophisticated analysis will also help for a satisfactory solution of the policy issue of the present study.

The order of discussions of Chapter IV will be as follows: In section 4.1 some questions on methodology appropriate to the analysis of multivariate problems are discussed. A specific multivariate methods have been used in the present study and it will therefore be useful to discuss at the outset their important features and their relationship with some of the possible alternative methods.

Section 4.2 presents the findings based on simple correlation analysis. It is mainly presented for the purpose of illustration and used as a step for clarifying the need for multivariate approach. A detailed discussion on the variables used in the multivariate context given in section 4.3 and section 4.4 provides the findings and interpretation of the results. The main points of this chapter are summarised in section 4.5.

4.1 Some Notes on the Methodology of Multivariate Analysis and Sample

There are a number of different approaches to the multivariate problems posed above. In particular the following four widely used approaches can be identified :

(1) R.A. Fisher's discriminant analysis, (2) Mahalanobis generalised distance analysis, (3) Hotelling's T^2 and generalised analysis of variance and (4) The regression analysis and linear probability functions. Although these various approaches have distinct historical origins, deriving from different ways of looking at these problems but they are also closely interrelated. There is little scope in the present study of discussing various characteristics and the nature of the interrelationship that exists among the approaches. The next section will identify the reasons for preferring regression analysis approach in exclusion of others.

The regression equation model can be stated in the following way:

$$y = \beta_0 + \beta_1 X_1 + \beta_2 X_2 + \ldots \beta_k X_k + \Sigma$$

Where Bo, B_1, B_2... B_k are the regression coefficients to be estimated and y is the dependent variable and X_1....X_k are the independent variables.

Then if E (E) = 0

$$E\,[\,Y/X\,] = \beta_0 + \beta_1 X_1 + \beta_2 X_2 + \ldots \beta_k X_k$$

where X is the matrix of observations on the regressors. In other words the value of y, calculated from the fitted linear regression equation, can be regarded as an estimate of the conditional probability of y given the x values. This is indeed a useful way of looking at the problem, but the approach suffers from two important drawbacks :

(a) The assumption of homoscedasticity which is made in the classical regression model becomes untenable when the dependent variable Y is dichotomous.

(b) In principle it is quite possible for the value y above, calculated from the linear regression equation, to be greater than 1 or less than O.[1]

Inspite of the above drawbacks, for the present investigation regression approach has been adopted because of its clear commonsense interpretation, wide use and scope of direct application to the problems under consideration. With the help of this approach, it would be possible to find out to what extent, if at all, control criteria influences the economic behaviour of management controlled firms.

Most of the earlier studies of similar nature relied on any of the statistical approach described above and naturally used published data for the purpose of their analysis. A quite different approach based on interview has been adopted in a number of studies with limited scope. The objective of all these studies was to find out the source of managerial satisfaction and objectives of their company, in order to test, growth - profitability controversy raised by managerial theory.[2] The primary objective of the present section of the study is to identify to what extent the separation of ownership from control can be identified as a determinant of inefficient functioning of management controlled firm. It lays little emphasis on how the objective of the firms change with control type.[3] Keeping in view the primary objective of the study, it is believed, efficiency consequences of separation of ownership from control, considering a number of variables, can be measured objectively on the basis of accounting information. This information can be treated as an end result that measures accurately the attitude of the managers towards their firms.

Apart from the methodological issues involved in the present section, it is further necessary to have a clear discussion on the sample firms under consideration. First of all, industry structure is an important determinant that can influence the economic performance of the firm. To account for this inter-industry differences, as in the earlier chapter, mainly three industries have been considered in the present section, such as Textile, Engineering and Chemicals. Secondly, in order to find out whether inefficiency of the management controlled firm can be explained in terms of separation of ownership from control, some owner controlled firms belonging to these three industries were considered along with the original sample. While identifying a firm as owner controlled, again the study depends upon the definition provided by Securities Contracts Regulation Act for identifying the real owner of the business. Apart from interest group equity holding, composition of the board of directors, the extent to which the large owners held executive position - all these information were considered to ascertain whether the dominant shareholders actually enjoy "active control" in the business or not. It means the sample included the firms where equity holding of the largest interest group equal to or are more than 25% and where there is the clear evidence that the "active control" lies with the owner.

While selecting the sample for owner controlled firm further two criteria were considered. Firstly, the firm must be a member of the top 250 companies of India, at least at any point of time under consideration (1979-83). Secondly, institutional equity holding in the firm should not exceed 20 per cent. This cut off rate though fixed up arbitrarily, was imposed in order to minimize the chance of misclassification between two groups of firm due to increase in institutional holding during the period of time under study. Applying all these criteria ultimately 9 firms each belonging to textile and chemical 10 for engineering were selected for further analysis. Nature of the sample firms under consideration now stands as follows:

Table 4.1

Distribution of Sample Firm

	Owner	*Management*	*Total*
Textile	9	11	20
Chemical	9	16	25
Engineering	10	23	33

In the regression analysis these two groups of firms were identified by using dummy variables - 0 for firms having institutional holding below 20%, 1 for firms having institutional holding 25% and above.

4.2 Simple Correlation Analysis : Results - Some Issues for Discussions

Table 4.2 presents the simple correlation coefficient between different performance criteria used throughout the study such as, profit, growth, earnings to equity, valuation and control as independent variable. The table is mainly provided for illustration purpose and used as a step for further discussions. However, the results may be considered along with the findings based on sophisticated analysis carried on in the latter part.

Table 4.2

Simple Correlation Coefficients

Correlation between	*Chemicals*		*Textile*		*Engineering*	
	N=25		*N=20*		*N=33*	
	r	*t value*	*r*	*t*	*r*	*t*
1. Profit rate and control	-.394	-1.91[c]-	-.226	-.90	-.347	-1.96[c]
2. Growth rate and control	.030	-	-.581	-2.85[b]	.106	.573
3. Earnings to equity and control	-.922	-9.7[a]	.032	-	-.158	-.814
4. Valuation and control	-.310	-1.8[c]	-.515	-2.32[b]	-.122	-.62

Level of significance - (a) 1% level (b) 5% level, (c) 10% level.

Table 4.2 presents the simple correlation co-efficients between different performance criteria and type of control as independent variable for three industries. Observations are not complete due to non-availability of relevant information for all the variables of the sample firms included in each industry. So within each industry a number of firms vary slightly for each variable and this is mainly applicable for earnings to equity and valuation.

Although it is difficult to make a strong case for anything on the basis of zero-order correlation analysis, the bits of evidence presented in table 4.2 can be summarized as follows : -

(1) Chemicals and Engineering show a particular pattern of behaviour than that of textile. Findings relating to textile industry are to be considered with reservation. Out of the total number of observations of 20 companies in textile industry, 11 belong to management control firm. All these firms are engaged in cotton textile industry. Due to paucity of firms fulfilling all the criteria for selection, owner controlled firms numbering 9, include some firms that belong to Jute textile & Woollen textile. Though all these industries (Cotton, Jute, Woollen & Rayon textile) very conveniently can be grouped under the broad heading "Textile industry", obviously industry structure for all these industries are different and it might be a possible source of bias in the findings.

(2) In chemical and engineering-profit rate, earnings to equity and valuation is negatively correlated with institutional holding. For chemical this relationship is statistically significant at 1% level for earning to equity, for profitability and valuation they are significant at 10% level. For engineering the relationship is statistically significant at 10% level only for profit rate. For these two industries, growth rate is positively correlated with institutional holding, but is never statistically significant at 10% or better level.

(3) For textile industry, profit rate, growth and valuation are negatively correlated with institutional holding, whereas for earnings to equity sign of coefficient is positive but not statistically significant.

(4) Considering a number of variables, inefficiency of management controlled firm can fairly be explained in the perspective of separation of ownership from control. To put it in other way, for a number of variables owner controlled group of firms belonging to the same industry outperform the management controlled firms

by a considerable margin.

(5) The table also provides a crude impression that the hypothesis regarding the behaviour of management controlled firms that have been developed in Chapter II can be confirmed. It may be recalled that the hypothesis were formulated on the basis of the theoretical foundation on "managerial capitalism" developed by earlier authors like Baumol,[4] Williamson,[5] Marris[6] etc. The findings of the present empirical study have a close similarity with the earlier studies conducted in the developed countries by Monsen et al,[7] Radice[8] etc.

(6) The analysis further gives an impression that very rightly institutional owned firms have been identified as management control firms. Thanks to the passive nature of financial institutions that permits management with insignificant equity holding to exert "active control" over firms and characteristics associated with management control predominate on these firms.

The main problem with the analysis is, it assumes type of control is the only variable that influences performance criteria selected for the study. Apart from control, a number of other variables mainly related to market structure and size also influences the performance of the firm. So the statistical technique to be adopted must be capable of distinguishing the effects of these different variables on the performance of the firm. So that differences due to high and low equity holding of financial institutions could be identified properly. After careful consideration, the variables other than control that might effect each performance criteria have been selected and discussed below.

4.3 Selection and Discussions on Variables for Multiple Regression

Apart from control other determinants of profit rate mainly relate to market structure and size. Market structure basically deals with the monopoly power. High concentration ratio and high barriers to entry are expected to be associated with high profits since such concentration or barriers allow control over market prices. Large market share in general is expected to yield high profitability - (1) by giving the firm a share-based product differentiation advantages, (2) by providing opportunities to the firm to operate in oligopolistic group for some joint strategies and increase in its bargaining power. Since both concentration and barriers to entry may be considered as an explanatory variable of profit rate. Findings of empirical study showing the relationship between these two variables and profit rate is however contradictory. So the nature and extent of relationship that might exist between these variables is still open to question. A brief discussion on some of the representative studies in this context would be in order.

Bain,[9] Mann,[10] Schwartzman[11] have empirically demonstrated that barriers to entry and concentration ratios apparently exert independent (and significant) influences on rates of return. Again findings of Bain[12] and Schwartzman[13] was disputed by Stigler.[14] He found no relationship between profitability and four firm concentration ratio in the three digit U.S. manufacturing industries for the years 1947 to 54. In the Indian context also, there are contradictory evidences. Study of Katrak[15] is worth mentioning in this respect. He found that high concentration is associated with lower profitability. It was argued that highly concentrated industries being subjected to high degree of antimonopoly regulation and, at the same time, probably, because of great 'X - inefficiency', had shown lower profitability as compared to the industries having moderate degrees of concentration. In contrast, Sawhney and Sawhney[16] found that profit rate is directly related to concentration in a large number of industries. Further, very interestingly, no conclusive result emerged from the study of Gupta[17] about the relationship between profit rates and barriers to entry.

The major problem one has to face while incorporating market structure as an explanatory variable of profit rate that of the firms being classified into industries at the level

(2 digit or 3 digit) for which such measures are available. The main difficulty is that firms and particularly large firms, frequently do not fit neatly into a particular industry. Using a 3 digit classification involves including many firms much of whose activities lie outside those industries to which they are classified, while a 2 digit classification includes a wide variety of market types in terms of both structure and demand growth.

An alternative approach to combat this problem to a limited extent is to make industry wise calculation to pick up inter industry differences.

Size as a determinant of profitability is again open to question. There are at least several contradictory studies that could be used to predict the likely consequences of using this variable. First of all Hall and Weiss[18] found, "size does tend to result in high profit rates as Baumol proposed".[19] Again the hypothesis was rejected by the studies of Steklers,[20] Samuels and Smith.[21] Further Singh and Whittington[22] in the context of U.K. industries found no systematic relationship between profit and size. It is noteworthy in all these studies that size has been measured either on the basis of net assets employed or sales.

From the above mentioned discussions, regression equation considering profit rate as dependent variable may be stated in the following way : -

$$Yp = \beta_o + \beta_1 c + \beta_2 o + \beta_3 s + \beta_4 g + \Sigma$$

Where c = control type, o = opening asset size, s = opening sales, g = growth rate of assets.

(2) Turning to the second variable growth, it is obviously responsive to a number of factors other than the type of control, because investment opportunities differ greatly across the firms. One would ideally like to compare the actual growth rate in a firm with the rate that would maximize the firms present value, and then compare the magnitude of divergence between these two variables across control type. Since present value maximizing norm can not

be observed, contrast among actual growth rate must suffice. Previous researchers have assumed that firms within the same industry have similar investment opportunities. This assumption will be employed in the present analysis also.

Apart from industry characteristics and control, other determinants of growth rate that have been considered in the study as explanatory variable are profit rate and size. It is difficult to establish a precise relationship between profit rate and growth because of their simultaneous nature i.e., profitability depending on growth on one side and growth depending on profitability on the other. Yet Singh and Whittington[23] by making a priori simplification that growth depends on profitability, found the relationship positive and significant for the firms. This simplified assumption has been followed in the present study also.

Further, the empirical finding is inconclusive so far as the relationship between size and growth rate is concerned. Samuels,[24] Singh and Whittington[25] found larger firms grow at a faster rate than the smaller firms. On the other hand there is a well known thesis that small units find it easier to make big percentage increases than do large units. It was further empirically confirmed by the studies of Kamarschen.[25] In all the studies where size has been considered as an explanatory variable of growth rate, it has been measured either on the basis of net assets or sales at the beginning year of the study.

Regression equation considering growth as dependent variable and several explanatory variables incorporating the essence of above discussions may be stated as follows : -

$$Y_g = \beta_o + \beta_1 C + \beta_2 O + \beta_3 p + \Sigma$$

Where C = control type, O = opening asset size, P = profit rate.

3) It has already been mentioned in Chapter II, that in many of the earlier studies, earnings to equity has been used to measure efficiency of the firm instead of profit rate. Obviously earnings to equity has a direct relation with profit

rate.[27] Apart from industry characteristics and control type that might effect profit rate, thereby earnings to equity, there is another important determinant that surely effects earnings to equity that is debt/equity ratio. Even when profits of two companies are identical, due to difference in capital structure earnings available to equity may be different. In the present study leverage ratio has not been considered as an explanatory variable of earnings to equity. It has been assumed that within an industry firms generally follow a patterned capital structure.

Regression equation considering earnings to equity as dependent variable may be stated in the following way -

$$Ye = \beta_o + \beta_1 c + \beta_2 S + \beta_3 g + \beta_4 P + \Sigma$$

Where C = control type, S = opening sales, g = growth rate of assets, P = profit rate.

It may be noted as earnings to equity is directly related with the profit rate, the explanatory variables that are used for profit rate almost have been retained here.

4) According to the theory of finance "Value" of share depends upon its future earning potentiality. As the future earning is not known, past earning is considered to predict the future. So earnings per share can be treated safely as a determinant of valuations. Further, growth of the company on which future pattern of profitability and earning to equity is associated has also been considered in the equation. It is worth mentioning at the present stage that there are so many factors that might influence the value of share, it is very difficult to identify specifically all of them. Moreover, the quality of value that ultimately emerges in the stock market depends heavily on the efficiency of the market in terms of its ability to value share properly. Regression equation considering valuation ratio as dependent variable is shown below :

$$yv = \beta_o + \beta_1 C + \beta_2 g + \beta_3 E + \Sigma$$

Where C = control type, g= growth rate, E = earning to equity.

A detailed description of the list of variables employed in the study is given below : -

List of Variables Employed

1. C = Type of ultimate control, O when individual or group holding is equal to or above 25% or owner controlled firm, 1 when institutional holding is equal to or above 25% or management controlled firm.

2. O = Opening asset size, that is total assets of the firm at the beginning year of the study i.e. 1979.

3. S = Net sales of the firm at the starting year (i.e. 1979) of the study. Variables 2 and 3 are mainly used to measure size of the firm.

4. g = Compounding growth of total assets of firm during the period 1979-83.

5. p = Average pretax rate of return on total assets of firm (1979-83) unweighted.

6. E = Average rate of return (after tax and preference dividend) on net worth (equity capital + Reserve and surpluses) unweighted.

7. v = Mean ratio of Book value to market value (average of high and low) for the time period (1979-83).

From the above list, a number of variables in different combinations have been used as explanatory variables for each efficiency measurement variable. It may be noted in some of the regression, sales revenue either independently or along with opening asset has been used to measure size and considered as an explanatory variable. For the present study sales revenue as a "size" or "scale" variable is not given much credence due to the following reasons. First of all, any regression involving sales (i.e. total revenue) as an explanatory variable when profits (or total revenue minus total cost) in any form, appear as the dependent variable contains a positive spurious correlation, since the identical variable (total revenue) appears on both sides of the equation. Secondly, multicollinearity is likely to be a problem - i.e. high inter correlation among the independent variables - in most of the multiple regressions involving sales. Finally, the economic importance of a firm is measured by what it contributes to the national income and to count the contribution of its suppliers is simply double (or multiple) counting. Value added is a correct flow measure of firm size, just as assets are a correct stock measure. Since the relationship between profit rate and sales has been subject to investigation by a number of writers, the sales revenue variable is retained with skeptic attitude. It is made available for those who are favourably inclined toward its value.

It is obvious from the above discussions that the study favours total asset as a measure of size. It is consistent with the view of Hall and Weiss[28] who strongly supported Baumol's thesis that there are "substantial" capital requirement barriers - i.e. size tends to result in high profit rates. Since Baumol defined size in formulating his size - profit hypothesis as the amount of owned and borrowed money capital, total assets are probably a good approximation.

4.4 Multiple Correlation Analysis and Interpretation of the Results

Within the single-equation least squares method relied on in the present study, the analysis now may be extended by employing multivariate statistical techniques. These results, which are probably more important than those of the table 4.2 are presented in table 4.3.

Table 4.3

Multiple Correlation Coefficients Relating Different Performance Indicators to Various Explanatory Variables

(A) Profit as Dependent Variable

Partial Coefficients of Determination r^2 and (t values) of

Industry	*Equation Number*	*C*	*O*	*S*	*g*	*P*	*E*	*R* (RV)	*F*
N = 25	1	-.293	-.357	.368[c]	.02			.529	1.943
Chemicals		(1.375)	(1.710)	(1.771)				(.279)	
Textile	2	-.555[b]	.399	-.417[c]	.843[a]			.857	10.398[a]
N = 20		(2.586)	(1.689)	(1.781)	(6.075)			(.734)	
Engineering	3	-.402[b]	.207	-.183	.325[c]			.49	2.215[c]
N = 33		(2.326)	(1.122)	(.986)	(1.818)			(.24)	

Growth as Dependent Variable

Industry	*Equation Number*	*C*	*O*	*S*	*g*	*P*	*E*	*R* (RV)	*F*
Chemicals	4	.216	-.253			.333		.394	1.287
N = 25		(1.016)	(1.201)			(1.618)		(.155)	
Textile	5	-.644[a]	.06			.780[a]		.855	14.731[a]
N = 20		(3.369)	(.241)			(4.991)		(.732)	
Engineering	6	.174	.078			.299[c]		.335	1.222
N = 33		(.953)	(.426)			(1.690)		(.112)	

Industry	Equation Number	C	O	S	g	P	E	R (RV)	F
		Partial Coefficients of Determination r^2 and (t values) of							
Earnings to Equity as Dependent Variable									
Chemicals	7	-.861(a)		.269	.647(a)	.206		.957	47.033(a)
N = 25		(6.993)		(1.151)	(3.5)	(.873)		(.915)	
Textile	8	.180		-.471(c)	.0671	.614(b)		.831	7.816(a)
N = 20		(.687)		(1.997)	(.252)	(2.916)		(.69)	
Engineering	9	-.150		.366(b)	.189	.508(a)		.667	5.217
N = 33		(.777)		(2.01)	(.985)	(3.00)		(.444)	
Valuation as Dependent Variable									
Chemicals	10	-.335			-.125		.536(b)	.618	3.091(c)
N = 25		(1.378)			(.489)		(2.404)	(.381)	
Textile	11	-.461(c)			.007		.360	.626	3.224(c)
N = 20		(2.01)					(1.497)	(.391)	
Engineering	12	-.059			-.026		.301	.335	1.095
N = 33		(.304)			(.136)		(1.615)	(.112)	

* Level of significance : (a) = 1% level, (b) = 5% level and (c) = 10% level.

Before making any critical analysis of the above table, at the outset, it is to be mentioned, due to non-availability of information, the number of firms in each industry vary slightly for each variable. The following tentative conclusions based on the above table are suggested below.

(1) First of all, in general, the conclusions suggested by the simple correlation analysis in table 4.2 relating different performance indicators and types of control, remain unaltered in the multivariate analysis. There is only a very significant deviation from table 4.2 in the relation between profit and control in textile industry. Earlier it was negatively correlated, now it is not only positively correlated, the relationship is statistically significant at 5% level. It is not surprising because in the multivariate context nature and extent of relationship may change dramatically.

(2) While sales revenue has been included in some of the regression as an indicator of total size and is generally statistically significant but has been omitted for further discussions for the reasons stated above. Another measure of size is opening asset. Relationship between size and profitability, size and growth, is not straight forward but it is not surprising or inconsistent with the findings of earlier studies.

Coefficient showing the relationship between size and profit, size and growth for chemical industry shows a negative sign. It contradicts the finding of Hall and Weiss[29] that "size does tend to result in high profit rates". The view which has a more common sense appeal and it is difficult to rationalize the present findings. One way to interpret the result is, small units find it easier to make big percentage increases both in profit and growth rate than do large units. The type of arguments that have been offered by many of the earlier authors. The argument though not entirely satisfactory is based on the logic that a small firm has a greater growth opportunity than a big firm which has already reached a critical level, so a small firm, until it reaches that critical level, will grow faster than the big firm. Moreover, some type of managerial inefficiency is associated with size causing a decrease in the rate of return in comparison with small firms. However, the particular finding fits well with the result of earlier studies of Kamerschen,[30] Radice,[31] Singh and Whittington.[32]

In the case of Textile and engineering, profit and growth rate are positively related to size. The finding is more consistent and theoretically appealing. As a whole, size effect on profit or growth is insignificant, the value of the co-efficient is never statistically significant at 10% or better level.

(3) It has been mentioned earlier that there is a two way relationship between profit and growth. These two variables are positively correlated with one another and in many a cases the relationship is statistically significant at 10% or better level. It further confirms the findings of Singh and Whittington.[33]

(4) The relationship between earnings to equity (another measure of efficiency) to control shows a similarity in trend with the relationship between profit and control. For chemicals and engineering the sign of the coefficient is negative while in the case of textile it is positive. For chemicals the relationship is significant at 1% level. Moreover, as it has been expected, earnings to equity is positively correlated with profit and growth and in many a cases the relationship is statistically significant. Further, as a whole, regression result is also significant for this variable. It further confirms the assumption that within an industry firms generally follow a patterned capital structure. Hence profit rate is mainly determinant of return to equity and for the purpose of analysis capital structure may be ignored.

(5) In respect to valuation, results should to be accepted with reservation. The whole exercise is based on the assumption of perfect capital market. Valuation and

control for all the industries is negatively correlated and for textile it is significant at 10% level. The analysis further confirms the generally accepted view that earnings available to equity holders is the main determinant of market value of share. The relationship between growth and valuation is very weak.

(6) As a whole, the relationship between control and different performance variable, which is the main point of interest of the study, reveals that owner controlled group of firms (in other way where institutional holding is minimum) outperformed the management controlled firms (where institutional holding is substantial) by a considerable margin. The finding has a direct bearing on the main policy issue of the present study.

(7) In Chapter II, four hypothesis regarding the behaviour of management controlled firms were developed with the help of leading literatures on "Managerial Theory". For the sake of convenience they are briefly repeated here : -

H_1 - Management controlled firm will show a lower rate of return than owner controlled firm.

H_2 - Management controlled firms grow faster than owner controlled firms.

H_3 - Management controlled firms have a lower return on equity than owner controlled firms.

H_4 - The ratio of market value to book value will be lower for management controlled firm than it is for owner controlled firm.

The above table clearly reveals that chemicals and engineering show a particular type of economic behaviour that is different from textile. The fact which was also identified in table 4.2.

Chemicals and engineering completely confirms the hypothesis of "Managerial" theory in the Indian context. For these two industries the rate of return, return on equity and valuation ratio of management control firm is lower than that of owner controlled firms. Whereas it shows a higher growth rate than its counter-part. The situation may also be explained in the following way so as to relate the discussion with the main policy issue under consideration. In the management controlled firms though government controlled financial institution is the real owner of the business, which happens to be "knowledgeable and powerful" prefers to remain passive. As a result, managers of this firm with little equity holding function are almost free from dominant shareholders constraint and can behave in a way that might help to further their own goal in exclusion of the goal of the owners.

(8) The analysis further reveals that very rightly institutional owned firms have been identified as management controlled firms, managers of these firms with little equity holding practically enjoy active control over these firms due to the passive role of dominant shareholder i.e. financial institutions. As a result the behaviour of these firms has a close similarity with that of management controlled firms. The same conclusion was drawn from the findings of simple correlation analysis.

Findings relating to textile industry do not confirm the above hypothesis. However, for this industry also coefficient showing the relationship between control and valuation shows negative sign and it is statistically significant at 10% level. One should not be tempted from the finding of textile industry to conclude that no problem exists in the present corporate structure. Managerial and bureaucratic inefficiencies certainly do exist but inspite of this, performance of management control firm is better than that of owner controlled firm.

4.5 Conclusions

There is a clear indication from the findings of Chapter III that the performance of management controlled firm for a number of variables is worse than that of industry average. Non-parametric test of Chapter III provides a faint indication that at least profit rate decreases with increase in institutional equity holding within the management controlled firm. Findings of the present chapter confirms the conclusion arrived at Chapter III. It shows that corporate performance to a large extent is negatively correlated with institutional equity holding. As a result performance of the owner control firm is far better than that of the management controlled firm. The finding is directly related with the main policy issue of the present study.

The findings of the present chapter also confirms that the financial institutions do not behave like a real owner of the business even when they are the dominant shareholders. Managers of this firm function almost free from dominant shareholders constraint that permit them to further their own goal in exclusion of the goal of the owners. The obvious conclusion is, public money is not properly utilised by the managers of these firms.

NOTES AND REFERENCES

1. Ajit Singh, Takeover, Cambridge University Press, 1971, p. 94.
2. For an interesting study of this nature see Arthur Francis, "Company Objectives, Managerial Motivations and the Behaviour of Large Firms : An Empirical Test of the Theory of Managerial Capitalism". Cambridge Journal of Economics, 4, 1980, pp. 349-361.
3. It is a fact that the two issues are practically closely interrelated.
4. W.J. Baumol, Business Behaviour, Value and Growth, New York, 1959.
5. O.E. Williamsons, The Economics of Discretionary Behaviour, New Jersey, 1964.
6. R.L. Marris, The Economic Theory of Managerial Capitalism, London, 1964.
7. Monsen, Chiu and Cooley, "The Effect of Separation of Ownership and

Control on the Performance of the Large Firm" Quarterly Journal of Economics, August 1968, p. 435-451.

8. H.K. Radice, "Control Type, Profitability and Growth in Large Firms: An Empirical Study" The Economic Journal, September 1971, pp. 547-562.

9. J.S. Bain, "Relation of Profit Rate to Industry Concentration", Quarterly Journal of Economics, 65, 1951, pp. 293-324.

10. H.M. Mann, "Seller Concentration, Barriers to Entry and Rates of Return in 30 Industries, 1950-1960", Review of Economics and Statistics, 48, 1966, pp. 296-307.

11. David Schwartzman, "Effect of Monopoly on Price", Journal of Political Economy, 67, 1959, pp. 352-62.

12. J.S. Bain, op. cit., pp. 293-324.

13. David Schwartzman, op. cit., pp. 352-362.

14. G.J. Stigler, Capital and Rates of Returns in Manufacturing Industries, Princeton University Press, 1963.

15. H. Katrak, "Cost-Price Relationship in Indian Manufacturing Industries", The Journal of Development Studies, 17, 1980, pp. 62-79.

16. P. Sawhney and B. Sawhney, "Capacity Utilisation, Concentration and Price-Cost Margins : Results on Indian Industries", Journal of Industrial Economics, 21, 1973, pp. 145-53.

17. V.K. Gupta, "Cost functions, Concentration and Barriers to Entry in Twenty-Nine Manufacturing Industries of India" Journal of Industrial Economics, 17, 1968, pp. 57-72.

18. Hall and Weiss, "Firm Size and Profitability", Review of Economics and Statistics, August, 1967.

19. Baumols hypothesis is based on the idea that the large firms have all the alternatives available to small firms plus the investment options requiring capital on a scale sufficiently large so as to exclude small firms. The hypothesis of Baumol is not at all new, since it was put by J. Steindl (Small and Big Business : Economic Problems of the Size of Firms, Oxford, 1945). Steindl called this the asymmetry principle and developed it quite extensively.

20. H.O. Stekler, Profitability and Size of Firm, Berkeley, 1963.

21. J. Samuels, and D. Smith, "Profits, Variability of Profits and Firm Size", Economica, 35, 1968, pp. 127-139.

22. A. Singh and G. Whittington, Growth, Profitability and Valuations, Cambridge, 1968.

23. See Singh and Whittington, op. cit.

24. J. Samuels "Size and Growth of Firms", Review of Economic Studies, 32, 1965, pp. 105-12.

25. Singh and Whittington, op. cit.

26. D.R. Kamerschen, "The Influence of Ownership and Control on Profit Rates", American Economic Review, Vol. LVIII, June, 1968, pp. 432-445.

27. In perfectly competitive long run equilibrium, profit rates on equity, but perhaps not on say total capital or assets, should tend toward equality between industries.

28. M. Hall and L.Weiss - "Firm Size and Profitability", Review of Economics and Statistics, August, 1967, 49, pp. 319-31.

29. M. Hall and L. Weiss, op. cit., 1967.

30. D.R. Kamerschen, op. cit., 1968.

31. H.K. Radice, op. cit., 1971.

32. Singh and Whittington, op. cit., 1968.

33. Ibid.

CHAPTER FIVE

Conclusions and Policy Implications

Introduction

At least two major conclusions can be drawn from the empirical studies of the earlier chapters. First, with a rise in institutional equity holding, inefficiency of firm also increases. Corollary to this, the study further reveals that the performance of the firms, where institution by virtue of its large equity holding is the real owner of business, is worse than that of others. The findings have far reaching implications. Specially when it is believed that institutions have to come in a bigger way in future to supply necessary funds for the development of private corporate sector (See Appendix-IV). Funds invested by institutions may be regarded as public money. When there is clear evidence of misutilisation of public money, managerial exploitation of owners, the issue gets prominence - what steps should the institution take to prevent this malfunctioning so as to ensure better utilisation of resources?

5.1 Background Discussions

Before entering into any discussions regarding the steps to be taken by financial institutions in the present context, it would be in order to make it clear the environment under which management of Indian corporations function.

(1) Indian managers to a large extent are immuned from stock market discipline. A market that cannot provide necessary financial support to corporations also loses its significance as an "efficient allocator of resources" and "guardian of efficiency" - the two main economic functions of a stock market.

(2) Financial institutions, the real owner of the business, by their passive attitude permit management of the corporation to function freely.

(3) Inactive capital market that forces the firm to depend on internal savings further allows management to avoid capital market discipline.

(4) Small individual investors who are scattered and disorganised have little influence in the corporate power structure, hence can simply be ignored by the management of the corporation.

(5) Absence of fierce takeover battle like capitalist countries, permits even inefficient management to operate freely without any possible threat from their counterpart.

(6) Thanks to the doctrine of mixed economy that permits existing management with insignificant equity holding to behave like "owner" of the business and forces the real owner to behave like a spectator of the whole show.

Thus it appears, apart from divorce of ownership from control, there are other factors that have contributed significantly for the free functioning of the management of Indian corporate sector. The truth is, managers of Indian business function in a cosily sheltered and sedentary world insulated from any sort of threatening, pressure, accountability. The ultimate result is -

(1) The proportion of nondividend paying companies have

steadily gone up from less than 20 per cent in 1961 to more than 40 per cent in 80's and onwards. It shows that the board is increasingly failing to discharge their duties towards suppliers of risk capital (see Appendix V).

(2) The growing incidence of corporate sickness in India is a well known fact and needs no elaboration. Roughly, one out of every six among listed companies in India is a sick company. About 15-20 per cent of bank advances to the industrial sector are locked up in sick units and are a matter of considerable concern to governmental and banking authorities. Mismanagement and diversion of funds are the main reasons contributing nearly 52 per cent of the total causes of sickness in large units (see Appendix-VI and VII).

(3) Though international comparisons of incremental capital output ratios are tricky, but it is a fact, Indian corporate sector has one of the highest ratios among developing countries. There is one hypothesis[1] that this unusually high (and even rising) incremental capital output ratio, namely the effects of high investment are being partially cancelled by a low productivity of that investment. So effect of huge investment in corporate sector is not reflected in a respectable growth rate. Undoubtedly a major part of the general rise in capital-output ratio is attributable to the inefficiency in utilization and management of capital.[2]

(4) Default in respect of repayment of deposits and interest is also on the way of increasing. This may be treated as one of the primary functions of the board towards its suppliers of loan capital.[3]

Only few examples to substantiate the case of ineffective board functioning have been discussed here. There are also innumberable examples that may be cited in this respect.

Problems arising out of separation of ownership from control, soft attitude of individual and institutional investors, mismatching of authority and responsibility, resulting inefficient functioning of the board is not a unique feature of the Indian corporate sector alone. Even in industrially developed countries such as U.K. and U.S.A. The present board system is under severe attack now a days. It is often argued that declining thrust and productivity in these two countries is partially attributable to ineffectual board. Harold Geneen, former chief executive of the International Telephone and Telegraph Company of U.S.A. states the problem as follows - "under present conditions, shareholders, whether individual or institutions have virtually no way of knowing whether or not they are getting their money's worth from the men hired to manage their company... over the years they have grown so soft and so ineffectual that most often they are captive of management rather than effective representatives of the company owners...". He also argued "... the prime function of a board of directors is to form continuous judgements on whether or not the chief executive and his management team are running things properly" - present board system failed miserably in this respect. Geneen further opined that the present system of functioning of board, lack of strict regulations to control the management, wide gap between authority and accountability are the main reasons contributing towards ineffective functioning of the board and thus decline in productivity of American industry.[4]

Very rightly in India also for a long period of time, the present board system has come under severe attack from different corners. The way the board is formed by the controlling group giving it a nature of dummy character, their style of functioning, insufficient provision of the Companies Act to regulate undesirable activities of the management, lack of fair dealing and return to investor have all come under the perview of present criticism. The startling disclosure of Vivian Bose commission on the affairs of Dalmia Jain group and the discovery of serious mismanagement by certain other groups added fire to the fuel.

5.2 Change in the Attitude Needed

The above discussion makes it clear that the Indian situation is not completely unique; it has some similarities with industrially developed countries with some obvious exceptions. In capitalist countries with wide dispersal of shareholding, the investors, be it individual or institutional, have little significance in the corporate power structure and cannot exert any meaningful influence upon the management of the corporation. But in India, shareholding is concentrated in the hands of financial institutions, so opportunity is there to take both corrective and punitive action to control undesirable activities of the management. What is required is only a change in the present attitude of financial institutions and this change is desirable on two counts.

Firstly, the distinction between the so called "private" sector and "public" sector has become somewhat blurred with tremendous increase in equity holding of financial institutions. In a true sense[5] government controlled institutions are the real owner of business of a large number of private corporate sector. Under the situation, government as the real owner should not hesitate to enforce stricter discipline on existing management if it is needed.

Secondly, when the empirical study clearly reveals misutilisation of public fund by the present management, the situation demands that institutions should come forward to prevent it. Institutions (LIC/UTI) as a custodian of small investors can not remain mere spectators under the situation. If they do so they will be failing to discharge their responsibilities towards small investors.

Thus, both legal and economic situation demands an active participation of institutions in the management of the private corporate sector. The issue that is emphasized, that the owner must behave like an owner so that these firms can truly be called as "owner controlled" firm.

5.3 Steps to be Taken

To stop managerial exploitation of owners, two steps should be taken simultaneously - (1) Companies Act 1956 to be amended properly to make management more responsive towards investors, (2) Strict vigilance on the part of institutions is required to implement true the spirit of Companies Act. While the former will ensure that the management has to function within a well defined legal framework and the latter will provide the guarantee that the provisions of the act would be properly implemented only to uphold the interest of investors.

Companies Act is an instrument for regulating the conduct of the company management towards its shareholders and creditors, besides providing for certain minimum requirements necessary for an artificial person to conduct its affair. The Companies Act has been amended so many times that now it looks very complex. Experience shows that the controlling group very successfully use this law for their personal gain at the cost of those outside the system, be it shareholders, creditors, consumers.[6] This has partly been possible because of the noninterfering nature of shareholders including financial institutions. Thus management has been permitted the most blatant violations of the provisions of the Companies Act relating to prospectus, financial disclosure, intercorporate investments, managerial remuneration and restraints in dealing with organisation in which the management is interested. Thus, not only amendment of Companies Act is sufficient but a strict vigilance on existing management is essential on the part of institutions, the real owner of business.

Measures to be adopted by institutions in this respect may be clubbed very conveniently under two broad headings (1) corrective action (2) punitive action. While corrective action denotes remedial measures to be taken to streamline the activities of the present system so as to make it more efficient. Punitive action, on the other hand, means steps to be taken in the form of removal of existing management who did not care or failed to respond properly against the corrective action taken by institutions. Both the situations demand active participation of real owner in the management of the corporation.

5.4 Some Corrective Measures

(a) Steps to be taken for an Effective Participation by the Board of Directors in the Decision Making Process

The issue is emphasized because the central weakness of corporate boards in India has been their dummy character. This is widely admitted and has been subject of much sarcastic comment. The dummy character resulted from all board appointments being controlled solely by the controlling group of the company. The institution insists that the assisted companies must broad-base their boards by including professionals from various disciplines. The issue remains that the directors appointed under the broad-basing requirement still owe their allegiance to the controlling interest on whom their continuance depends. The ultimate result, according to Marris[7], - "corporation has been taken over by transcendent management, whose functions differ in kind from those of the traditional subordinate or "mere manager". These people... can yield considerable power without necessarily holding [substantial] equity, sharing profit, or carrying risk". This transcendent management has successfully been able to turn the board into a "watch dog" that watches the interest of the controlling group instead of looking after the interest of shareholders at large.

It is urgently required that steps have to be taken to transform the boards from rubber stamp or passive bodies to independent vigilant bodies. The composition, selection of board personnel, their allegiance and attitude has to be changed drastically. The institution as the major shareholder should take the lead role in this respect. Such as nominee directors as the representative of real owner of business should very carefully discharge their supervisory function over existing management. They should actively take part in the decision making process of the board so as to make the board function more effectively. Outside directors should not be regarded as mere ornaments lending prestige to the company but as those who can benefit the company with their knowledge. Obviously they will not owe any allegiance to the controlling group but to the real owner of the business. Automatic inclusion of the younger members of the controlling group in the board has to be stopped. All these would turn the controlling group into mere "manager" of the business, functioning under strict control and supervision of the board under the leadership of institution.

(b) Procedure for Maintaining Accounts and Audit Standards to be Improved

Procedure for maintaining account to be improved in order to make it more purposeful. In fact, the present system of maintaining account and audit instead of protecting the interest of investors, has become an effective tool of management to further their own interest at the cost of investors. Such as, minimum disclosure requirements for import of capital goods, purchase of components from foreign principals or family organisation, on the plea that law does not apply as the interested organisations are not Indian companies, provides an excellent opportunity to further the economic goal of managers in exclusion of owners. Again, revaluation of assets to inflate the net worth has become endemic, but depreciation on the higher value is not charged to current income. No one knows what economic sense this makes except for inflating the value of the assets and perhaps the share value in the market. Further, depreciation seems to be increasingly a residuary entry - writing back, writing down, conversion from one rate to another, all are practised to serve the management's need only. Managerial remuneration disclosure defies all logic and shareholders are not in a position to know the total cost of management. Out of many, only a few examples have been cited above to show how accounting has become an art either to camouflage the misdeeds of the management or to project a particular type of image best suited for the management. It is unfortunate that at different occasions of amendment of the Companies Act, the government failed to introduce some innovation in the matter of accountability including disclosure in annual reports.

Corollary to this, it is also essential to give the needed effort to assure increase in the audit standard. The audit that may be regarded as a primary means to prevent managerial exploitation of owners. It is both painful and surprising to note that concurrent auditors appointed by institutions in many a cases brought out irregularities, leakages, and accounting manipulations indulged in by some managements.[8] It seems that the audit profession does not bother about the security of the funds of the investing public. 'True and Fair' is no longer relevant in relation to company accounts. Some parts of the account may be true but what is important is that the major part should be fair to the family that is in the saddle. The reason is that the auditors consider the managements and not the shareholders as their employers thus the audit has become a mere formality.[9]

The situation demands that the nominee directors should have free access to a company's records, accounts and personnel to discharge their responsibility. Institutions on behalf of general shareholders may also think in terms of sueing the auditors for damages in such cases, which is a very common practice in developed countries. Further nominee directors can be instrumental in ensuring that the board gives attention to auditors objections, comments and suggestions. If nominee directors have any doubt regarding the standard of audit conducted by statutory auditor they may insist on formation of board's audit committee in which nominee directors will be represented.

Further steps might be taken for some sort of supervisory audit of the accounts by a committee of shareholders who are not members of the board. Shareholders' association should be recognised and permitted to effectively participate in meeting in a representative capacity with a right to speak and vote on behalf of all its members. It should be made mandatory that the annual report should be furnished to the association. In the absence of any such committee, initiative should now be taken by the institutional investors to subject the accounts to an independent scrutiny in which even the auditors should be closely examined. Institutional investors who are the most knowledgeable persons cannot shake off their responsibility in this respect in the name of "true and fair" certificate already issued by the auditors who are at the mercy of the management.

Though technically the shareholders are expected to scrutinise the annual report of the directors and approve them by a formal motion, in practice shareholdings are diffused and shareholders often do not have the capability to match wits with those in power so that the adoption of the company's accounts by shareholders at the annual general meeting is merely a formality and often a farce. Justification of alert attitude of nominee directors so far as the preparation of accounts and audit is concerned lies here.

(c) Strict Restrictions and Vigilance on Intercorporate Investment is Necessary

There can hardly be any dispute over intercorporate investment when it is made out of genuine surpluses and with an aim to achieve benefit of diversification for the interest of the shareholders. However, there is an important issue that is often neglected - a company having raised funds under one charter cannot be the instrument for raising funds for another adventure of the controlling group. Yet these are the very principles that have been trampled upon for many a years even at the cost of the investors. In fact, the main problem with this type of investment lies elsewhere. The way and the purpose for which this investment is made nowadays, made it a subject of wide range of criticism. At present intercorporate investments have become an instrument for expanding family empires and a source of various misdeeds of existing management. There are various provisions U/S 372 of the Companies Act to regulate intercorporate investments and loans to protect the interest of shareholders and creditors from uncontrolled diversion of funds in the name of diversification. Administrative experiences show lack of willingness of existing management to abide by the true spirit of the act and insufficiency of the provisions to compel the unwilling management to behave properly in this respect.

This type of uncontrolled siphoning of funds by the promoter is one of the major causes contributing towards industrial sickness in India. It would be unrealistic to expect much from nominee directors in this respect. The reason is that board level is somewhat remote in the sense that boards have no contact with management level below it and have to depend entirely on information fed to them by chief executives. However, if nominee directors have any doubt regarding desirability or otherwise of the investment, in these cases also, they may insist on forming an audit subcommittee. The nominee director will obviously be a member of this committee from which the chief executive will be excluded. The Audit committee will conduct the audit absolutely free from any influence of the company's chief executive. Further, nominee directors should be given ample opportunity to have free access to the company's records, accounts and documents so as to help them to take judicious decision in this respect.

Another step, of course it requires change in the provisions of the Companies Act, may be helpful to discourage uncontrolled diversion of funds of promoter group to expand their family empires. The course involves, it is shareholders and not the board of directors who will decide upon their representatives in the company where investment has been made. So long as the board is not properly constituted as mentioned earlier, it would provide some leverage to the financial institutions so far selection of company representative is concerned. It would obviously discourage the existing management from uneconomic intercorporate investment.

(d) Payment to Directors and Certain Employees Including Perquisites should be Qualified in Monetary Terms and shown separately in the Accounts

Managerial remuneration is a well discussed subject which is very close to the heart of the so called professional managers. It is time that the provisions of the Companies Act with regard to managerial remuneration are completely withdrawn and the directors are asked to seek the shareholders' consent year after year for the total remuneration to be drawn by them. Perquisites, if possible, should be totally abolished. If the tax incidence has to be reduced, let the tax law be amended to provide for lower tax on honest persons who declare all their income and not camouflage their income in the name of perquisites.

Institutions which have major shareholdings can at least enforce some of the disciplines pending such an amendment to the law. There are some managerial malpractices that generally fall outside the ambit of audit. They are 'propriety' type such as extravagant top management perquisites, maintenance of luxurious guest houses when the company has been losing heavily etc. Nominee directors should keep a close watch on it so as to stop creation of a dreamworld at the cost of the shareholders.

Company Law Amendment Committee had categorically stated that in applying the ceilings on managerial remuneration and in the matter of disclosure, the actual cost should be ascertained irrespective of any provision in the taxing statues. In practice managerial remuneration disclosure defies all logic. It demands strict vigilance of nominee directors for accurate valuation of perquisites and their proper disclosure to the shareholders so that shareholders can understand their total cost of management.

•

(e) The Law Board should be given the Right to Order Investigation into any Affairs of the Corporations

Along with this right to order investigation, the Company Law Board should be given the right to direct the removal of auditors who failed to discharge their duties properly. In fact this should be followed up with a provision for debarring such auditors from practice notwithstanding anything contained in the Chartered Accountants' Act.

It is also necessary that the present guideline should be changed and nominee directors should be given authority to insist on investigation relating to any matters of the corporation. To carry out this investigation the nominee director should be given authority to take help of professionals from outside the company. The reason is, it is nominee directors who are well informed about the functioning of the companies, can smell any wrong at an early stage and should be given the right to make arrangement for investigation.

Very close to the present issue, shareholders must be informed about the disallowance by the tax authorities of expenditure incurred by the company due to insufficient justification or in excess limits prescribed by the tax authorities. It is well known that a large part of the company's expenditure is incurred by way of what are known as vouchers, but they never find any mention in any auditor's report. All such expenditure incurred should be subject to the strictest scrutiny from the point of view of their relevance to the company's business. Uncontrolled diversion of funds for helping friends, creating an image of the management at the cost of investors needs to be examined strictly on the basis of the principle of ultra vires. Nominee directors should keep pressure on auditors for proper disclosure of all these information to the shareholders.

(f) Recognition of Shareholders Association, Change in the Definition of Officer etc.

Nominee director has nothing to do with the following suggestions, it requires government initiative so as to change the provisions of the Act in order to make management more responsive. It includes recognition of shareholders association, change in the narrow definition of officer so as to include all directors in its ambit. As long as these changes are not made institutional representatives will have to shoulder a larger responsibility of protecting the interest of investors.

It is expected that if the institutional representatives discharge their above role efficiently it will help to minimize managerial exploitation of owners. The role mentioned above may be described as a "watch dog" function of institution. Many more functions of above nature may be included in the list specially that which relates to payment of government dues in the form of excise, custom and other statutory dues, dues to the institutions and banks etc.

Apart from the above "watch dog" function, it is expected that the nominee directors should play a positive role in improving productive efficiency and quality of decision making by boards. Nominee directors should insist on matters relating to preparation of plan and review of plan etc. to be discussed thoroughly in the board. They should provide a constant pressure on management for showing better results. Nominee directors, if they have the requisite competence, may offer their expertise knowledge so as to improve decision making quality of board. Job description of nominee directors in this respect should include the following -

(1) Development of long term objectives as to profitability, growth, technology and organisational change;

(2) Review of the company's annual operating plan;

(3) Periodical review of performance against policies, objective and plan;

(4) Identification of major deficiencies in performance and underlying causes.[10]

5.5 Crux of the Problem

It is a fact, that financial institutions gradually changed their attitude towards assisted companies so as to ensure greater accountability on the part of the management of the corporation. It was not the general practice of term financing institutions before 1970 to nominate their representatives on the boards of assisted companies except in problem cases. It was in 1970 following the report of Dutta Committee[11] that the government of India decided as a matter of general policy that the public financial institutions should appoint their nominee directors on the boards of all assisted companies where substantial financial assistance had been provided. Emphasis on the role of nominee directors is shifted from "friend, philosopher, guide" to "watch dog" function. A recent government guideline provides[12], "A nominee director should be vigilant and if any undesirable practice prevalent in the assisted companies, including any abuse by the promoter group of its powers and privileges, comes to his knowledge, he should promptly bring it to the notice of Board and nominating institutions". It also states, "the nominee directors should ensure that the tendencies of the companies towards extravagance, lavish expenditure and diversion of funds are curbed". In fact many of the above suggestions already have been included in the new guideline for nominee directors. This attitude is most welcome specially in the context of empirical findings. In reality, experience shows ultimate outcome is negligible.[13] It has only been able to improve 'outer' discipline in board's functioning i.e. observance of proper board procedures has surely improved. So far achievement of true spirit of different guideline is concerned, institutions have to move a long way. Certain specific examples may be cited to show how controlling group even after issue of different guidelines simply ignore institutional representatives while taking major policy decisions. Escorts, where institutional equity holding is roughly 53%, issued shares and debentures of Rs. 15 crore without consulting even the institution beforehand. Premier Automobile raised car prices without consulting company's board of which R.B. Punja, Chairman, I.D.B.I. was the nominee director. The most interesting example is Shaw Wallace where there were no institutional representatives at all in the board till 1985 despite 32 per cent collective equity holding of L.I.C. and U.T.I. As a matter of fact, the controlling interest of public financial institutions is generally used merely to take-over of 'sick' units or marginal units saddled with large losses. It appears that the guiding principle is, government should finance the private sector which simultaneously acts as the risk absorber of the last resort and a charitable hospital where the private sector can dump its sick units.

The main problem in implementing even the existing guideline of I.D.B.I. is state monopoly capital nexus. State monopoly capitalism combines the strength of big business and that of the state into a single mechanism whose purpose is to reallocate national income in favour of big business houses at the same time to protect their interest even at the cost of general public.[14] So long as this nexus will continue, there might be several high sounding guidelines but "these guidelines will hurt nobody".[15]

5.6 Take-over and Corporate Efficiency

In western countries, take-over is a popular means for rapid diversification and growth. It also provides a constant threat to the existing management so as to improve efficiency of the firm and thereby valuation ratio.[16] Thus steady increase in efficiency can only provide necessary guarantee to retain control over the company. In this sense, take-over may be considered as a punitive action against the existing management which fails to utilise resources efficiently entrusted to them. Applying this logic, one could expect a fierce take-over battle in many of the government "owned"[17] corporations of India. As empirical study reveals a large number of such corporations fail to achieve the standard valuation ratio. In fact, intensity of corporate take-over battle is not that acute in India. It is partly due to the attitude of institutions towards take-over and different rules and regulations prevailing in the country. The fact is, though many a corporations are objectively ripe for take-over, they not facing any threat from their counterpart thus successfully avoiding the punitive action that should be taken against them.

Very recently, Indian corporate sector witnessed intense take-over battle over a large number of companies.[18] Says S.S. Nadkarni, managing director I.C.I.C.I. "A variety of factors have accumulated to trigger the recent spate of take-overs. Division of family holdings and the consequent quarrels, increased liquidity due to corporate results in the last few years, the fact that large houses can take-over companies through investment corporations set up for the purpose, the disinvestment of foreign shareholdings by multinational corporations which are recession hit in their own countries, industrial sickness and financial trouble. All these have fuelled the surge in acquisitions".[19] The most interesting part is in many a cases huge amount of premium over the market price of the shares were offered for acquisition. It is justified only when there is unexploited resources and after takeover through increased efficiency future benefit would be higher than the price presently offered. Ignoring other factors, it can be assumed that greater the inefficiency in corporate sector more will be the intensity of corporate take-over. To put it in another way, greater the inefficiency more will be the need for taking punitive action against the existing management to replace them by one which is more efficient and can utilise the resources properly. Almost identical argument was offered by Swaraj Paul during his consecutive raid on some Indian companies.

In industrially developed countries take-over enjoyed active encouragement of the government to make the firm more competitive both at national and international level. Government policy acted as a catalyst throughout the industry and intensified merger activities in many a countries. Industrial reorganization Corporation (I.R.C.) of U.K., Institute de Development Industrial (I.D.P.) of France, Instituto per la Ricostruzione Industriale (I.R.I.) of Italy played an active role in business combination of those countries.[20] A take-over bid in India has different implications than elsewhere because of the large equity holding in the hands of the institutions. Even a disguised bid can be frustrated by the institutions if they are not in favour of the new management. Further by virtue of large holdings they are in a position even to induce take-over. Who will be in the driver's seat, in many a cases, now largely depend upon the attitude of the institution. So it is necessary that there should be a clear definition of the role of the financial institutions in a take-over bid.

5.7 Take-over and Role of Institutions

F.I.C.C.I. in their memorandum submitted to Narasimham Committee[21] practically urged the government to follow two distinct policies regarding take-over. It states, "as a general rule the institution should support existing managements unless the latter are found to be grossly deficient. This would bring about a compromise between independence of management and the rights of the institutions as shareholders".[22] However the term "grossly deficient" has never been explained in the memorandum. The statement further provides "The financial institutions should unreservedly support Indian management"[23] in the context of any take-over attempt by NRI. The views expressed by FICCI clearly reveals that their attitude towards NRI raider is much stricter and they demand "unconditional" support of institutions. When the raid involves Indian industrialists they are ready to provide some leverage to financial institutions. Experience shows, in the absence of strict guideline, influential industrialists got the support of the institution for a company takeover. Such as Goenkas built their business empire with successive take-over of different industries and enjoyed the full support of institutions. Applying this philosophy they are already dominant in rubber, tyres and tubes field. Chronologically they have acquired Ceat tyres, Philips Carbon Black, Dunlop, Bayer. All these companies are either horizontally or vertically related with tyre industries. Moreover, they have also entered into a big way in the biscuit industries by acquiring controlling interest of Britania Biscuits. In the same way, violating all norms, institutions tried to hand over India Cement to I.T.C. Limited. Another glaring example of institutional favouratism to big business is induction of Khaitans' in the management of Standard Battery depriving the controlling group on flimsy ground. F.I.C.C.I.'s liberal attitude when take-over involves Indian companies has special significance in view of the above experiences.

The question is how the demand of F.I.C.C.I. that financial institution should support the existing management in the context of take-over is tenable in the background of the empirical findings of the present study? Can the government provide a clean chit to the existing management that they wouldn't be removed even when there is clear evidence that the performance of "government owned" private sector is not satisfactory?

In fact in different take-over situations, institution played a dubious role and was subject to vehement criticism. Specially if one considers institutional role in take-over that involves NRIs e.g. Escorts, Shaw Wallace, it will be clear that the institution suffers from indecision, confusion and ultimate decision that was taken seems to be heavily influenced by a political factor, pull, push and not by economic considerations. Thus it is felt that a guideline has to be prepared based primarily on economic criteria to be followed by institution in take-over situation. It is admitted that it is very difficult to lay down detail guidelines that could direct institutional behaviour in a tricky situation like take-over. However, an attempt can be made to develop a basic policy to be followed by the institutions in this context. Once this policy is determined and it is known that the policy enjoys official blessing it might have a far reaching implications on the corporations where the institution is the largest shareholder.

The role of institution defined in Section 5.4 may be described as a "corrective" step that should be taken by institution to streamline the activities of the management. Change of management through direct or indirect support in take-over may be considered as a "punitive" tool available to the institution for replacement of the existing management which fails to respond properly against the corrective measure of institution. This will provide a constant threat on the existing management and ensure better utilization of public money. Narasimham Committee almost expressed the identical view while defining the role of institution in the context of take-over. The Committee [2A] endorses the view that "an essential aspect of competition in a modern industrial economy is managerial competition, which implies, among other things, take-overs and mergers. The operation of the overall mechanism governing take-overs and mergers and the discharge by the financial institutions of their functions in this regard, should be guided primarily by objectives of efficiency".

However, it is very difficult to provide an operational definition of the term "economic efficiency" and to develop principles on this basis to be followed by the institutions in take-over. The problem becomes easier when take-over involves sick units. There is a clear indication that whatever might be the reasons, if a unit is sick, it denotes that resources have not been utilised properly. As the major shareholder, financial institutions have rightly taken the initiative in many a cases to replace the existing management of sick units. A study of a number of situations would reveal that sick units were handed over to big business houses practically free of cost in the midst of vehement opposition from other shareholders. An interesting example in this respect is Mcdowell and Hindustan Polymers Ltd. However, the role of institutions in this respect is most welcome, specially when the benefit that might be available to the society if these units could be revived outweigh its cost in respect of monopoly power. In these cases also the institution must be alert to ensure that different reliefs and benefits that are being provided by institutions and government to the acquiring unit is truly used for the revival of sick units.

When take-over involves profitable unit, the factors to be considered before taking any decision by the institutions are many. While the threat of take-over provides a constant pressure on existing management and ensures better utilisation of resources, at the same time, it permits with little investment, expansion of business empire thereby concentration of economic power. It demands both social and economic factors are to be considered by the institutions while deciding upon take-over. Based on this framework and findings of the empirical studies, some suggestions are given below.

First, institutions should make it clear that the present take-over battle is a tussle to get control over government owned companies. So institutions cannot remain passive in the whole situation.

Second, empirical findings justify that threat of change in the management through take-over is to be used as a punitive tool available to the institutions to promote efficiency of government owned companies.

Third, under normal circumstances institution should obviously support the existing management. At the same time, if records show that the management was not faithful to their investors, institutions should not hesitate to replace them.

Fourth, any attempt by big business to acquire a smaller one simply to increase economic power should be discouraged by institutions as far as possible. However, the issue is also looked after by M.R.T.P. commission.

Fifth, every effort must be given by the financial institutions to stop false take-over attempt so as to make quick money.

Lastly, it would be the duty of financial institutions to look after the interest of minority shareholders. They will induce bidder to offer the same price to minority shareholders also, the principle that is often violated by the institution itself.

NOTES AND REFERENCES

1. For an emphasis on this issue see A.V. Desai, "Factors Underlying the Slow Growth of Indian Industry", Economic and Political Weekly, 1981, annual number, March.
2. P. Bardhan, The Political Economy of Development in India, Oxford University Press, 1984, p. 27.
3. See Thanyavur "Companies Act Amendment Bill", Economic and Political Weekly, December 26, 1987, pp. 2245-2249.
4. Quoted in L.C. Gupta "Nominee Director's Role and Impact" M.D.I. Management Journal, Vol. 1, No. 1, 1988, p. 41.

5. If one goes through strict legal connotations, institution is the real owner of business when their equity holding in a corporation is equal to or more than 25%. As the average equity holding of institutions is 26%, a large number of private corporate sector can effectively be controlled by government through institutions.
6. See Thanyavur, op. cit., pp. 2245-49.
7. Robin Marris, The Economic Theory of "Managerial Capitalism", Macmillan and Co. London, 1964, p. 4.
8. L.C. Gupta, "Nominee Director's Role and Impact", op. cit., p. 46.
9. For a nice discussion on this issue see Thanyavur, "Companies Act Amendment Bill", op. cit., 1987.
10. See L.C. Gupta, "Nominee Director's Role and Impact" op. cit., 1988.
11. Industrial Licensing Policy Enquiry Committee, 1969, New Delhi.
12. Industrial Development Bank of India (1986). Guidelines for the use of Nominee Directors, Bombay - 1.
13. L.C. Gupta, "Nominee Director's Role and Impact" op. cit., p. 51.
14. V.I. Lenin, Collected Works, Vol. 24, p. 403.
15. S.K. Goel, Quoted from India Today, March 31st, 1984, p. 115.
16. For a discussion see Chapter II.
17. Where institutional holding equal to or more than 25 per cent.
18. Such as the case of D.C.M., Escorts, Shaw Wallace, Dunlop, Standard Battery, Tiru Tea, Jokai Tea, etc.
19. Quoted from India Today, March 15, 1983, p. 96.
20. For a detailed discussions see Christopher Tugendhat, The Multinationals, Pelican, 1978, Chapter 4.
21. Memorandum to Narasimham Committee, F.I.C.C.I., New Delhi.
22. Memorandum to Narasimham Committee, op. cit., p. 15.
23. Memorandum to Narasimham Committee, op. cit., p. 16.
24. Committee to Examine the Principles of a Possible Shift From Physical to Financial Controls, New Delhi, p. 25.

Appendix - 1

Industrywise Percentage Distribution of Shareholding According to Category of Owners

Category of Owners	Individual	Financial Institutions	Govern- & semi-Government	Non financial institutions bodies	Others	Total
	1	2	3	4	5	6
Industry Group						
Group - I						
Agriculture and Allied Products -						
Tea Plantations	37.77	15.10	-	46.96	.17	100.00
Group - II						
Processing and Manufacture - Foodstuffs, Textiles, Tobacco and Products thereof of which : -	45.28	23.94	.72	29.56	.50	100.00
Sugar	54.24	25.24	.20	19.80	.52	100.00
Cotton Textile	48.36	22.67	.42	28.30	.25	100.00
Jute	24.59	29.83	.03	38.26	7.29	100.00
Group III						
Processing and Manufacture - Metals, Chemicals and Products thereof of which : -	33.20	24.66	1.80	40.20	.14	100.00
Aluminium	27.64	25.30	.24	46.82	-	100.00
Engineering	34.27	28.25	.90	36.45	.13	100.00
Chemicals	32.68	20.21	3.12	43.83	.16	100.00

(Cont'd) . . .

Category of Owners	*Individual*	*Financial Institutions*	*Government & semi-Government*	*Non financial institutions bodies*	*Others*	*Total*
	1	**2**	**3**	**4**	**5**	**6**
Group - IV						
Processing and Manufacture not elsewhere classified of which : -	36.10	32.76	2.22	28.55	.37	100.00
Cement	51.33	38.84	.96	8.35	.51	100.00
Rubber and Rubber Products	35.22	23.57	2.44	38.74	.03	100.00
Paper and Paper Products	26.10	39.59	3.75	30.07	.49	100.00
Group V						
Other Industries of which : -	47.01	29.99	1.06	21.65	.29	100.00
Trading	33.42	25.30	.97	40.16	.15	100.00
Shipping	57.42	30.57	.05	11.82	.14	100.00

(*Source :* R.B.I. Bulletin, February 1983, p. 81, abridged and rearranged).

Appendix - II

Change in the Share Ownership Pattern of U.S. Industries

	Individuals	*Insurance Co.*	*Investment Trust*	*Pension Fund*	*Industrial & Commercial Co.*	*Overseas*	*Charitable Institutions*	*Government*	*Unit Trust*	*Total*
1963	58%	11%	9%	7%	5%	4%	3%	2%	1%	100
1983	25%	22%	6%	29%	5%	4%	2%	3%	4%	100

(*Source :* The Economist, 14-20 July 1984, Survey - 9).

Appendix - III

Pattern of Ownership by Size of Holdings

Category of Owners	1 Individual		2 Financial Institutions		3 Joint Stock Companies		4 Trust and Charitable Institutions		5 Govt. and Semi govt. bodies		6 Others		7 Total	
Size Range of Holding	Value	% of Total Share-holding of resp. Categories	Value	% of Total Share-holding of resp. Categories	Value	% of Total Share-holding of resp. Categories	Value	% of total Share-holding of resp. Categories	Value	% of total Share-holding of resp. Categories	Value	% of total Share-holding of resp. Categories	Value	% of total Share-holding of resp. Categories
Small = Rs. 1 Rs. 25000	37564.30	71.87	137.75	.39	343.29	.73	76.42	4.50	3.82	.18	59.71	16.32	38185.38	27.45
Medium = Rs. 25001 Rs. 50000	3579.61	6.85	120.45	.34	192.32	.41	78.76	4.64	2.44	.12	14.66	4.01	3988.24	2.87
Large = above Rs. 50000	11119.68	21.28	35461.02	99.27	46426.02	98.86	1541.95	90.86	2071.37	99.70	291.48	79.61	96911.52	69.68
	52263.68	100.00	35719.22	100.00	49661.63	100.00	1697.13	100.00	2077.63	100.00	365.85	100.00	139085.14	100.00
		37.58		25.68		33.77		1.22		1.49		.26	Percentage of Total	

(Source : R.B.I. Bulletin, February, 1983 p. 76 abridged and rearranged).

Appendix - IV

Amount of Resources that will have to be provided by the Financial Institutions

Year	*Expected Investment upto the end of Eighth plans (Rs. Crores) assuming a growth rate in investment @ 5.6% **			*Assistance that will have to be provided by Financial Institutions*		
	at 1981-82 prices	*@ 5% inflation*	*@ 10% inflation*	*at 1981-82 prices*	*@ 5% inflation*	*% 10% inflation*
1981-82	4830	4830	4830			
1982-83	5072	5326	5580			
1983-84	5356	5905	6480			
1984-85	5656	6547	7528			
1985-86	5973	7259	8744	2090	2540	3060
1986-87	6307	8049	10157	2207	2817	3555
1987-88	6661	8925	11799	2331	3124	4130
1988-89	7034	9896	13706	2462	3463	4797
1989-90	7427	10973	15921	2600	3840	5572
1990-91	7843	12167	18494	2745	4258	6473
1991-92	8282	13491	21482	2899	4722	7519
1992-93	8746	14958	24954	3061	5235	8734
1993-94	9236	16586	28986	3232	5805	10145
1994-95	9753	18391	33670	3413	6437	11784

(Estimated from the information available in Memorandum to Narsimham Committee, submitted by F.I.C.C.I., p. 5).

* The rate has been estimated by Rangarajan Committee.

Appendix - V

Percentage of Large Medium-Sized Companies not Paying Equity Dividend in Selected Years

Year	*Percent of Companies*
1961	18.8
1966	21.6
1971	26.9
1976	37.9
1980-81	40.0

Appendix - VI

Causes of Sickness	Percent to Total
(A) Mis-management including diversion of funds, infighting, lack of marketing strategy	52
(B) Faulty initial planning and other technical drawbacks	14
(C) Labour trouble	2
(D) Market recession	23
(E) Other reasons (power-cuts, shortage of raw materials, etc.)	9
	100

Source : The Economic Times, September 11, 1988.

Appendix - VII

Large Sick Units and Outstanding Bank Credit

	Year	No.	Amount of Outstanding Bank Credit (Crores)
	1980	409	1342.5
	1981	422	1478.8
	1982	444	1790.6
	1983	491	2014.3
	1984	545	2330.1
	1985	637	2980.2
(End June)	1986	689	3239
" "	1987	1712	4195.6

(*Source* : Economic Times, May 18, 1989).

Select Bibliography

Bain, J.S. "Relation of Profit Rate to Industry Concentration ". *Quarterly Journal of Economics*, 65, (1951).

Bardhan, P. *The Political Economy of Development in India.* Oxford University Press, 1984.

Baumol, W.G. *The Stock Market and Economic Efficiency.* New York, 1965.

Baumol, W.J. *Business Behaviour, Value and Growth.* New York, 1959.

Berla and Means. *The Modern Corporation and Private Property.* Macmillan, New York, 1932.

Desai, A.V. "Factors Underlying the Slow Growth of Indian Industry". *Economic and Political Weekly*, March, (1981).

Donaldson, Gordon. *Corporate Debt Capacity.* Boston, 1961.

Gupta, L.C. "Nominee Directors Role and Impact". *Management Journal*, M.D.I. Vol. I, No. I, January, (1988).

Gupta, V.K. "Cost functions, Concentration and Barriers to Entry in Twenty-Nine Manufacturing Industries of India".

Journal of Industrial Economics, 17, (1968).

Hall and Weiso. "Firm Size and Profitability". *Review of Economics and Statistics*, August, (1967).

Holl, Peter. "Effect on Control Type on the Performance of the

Firm in the U.K." *The Journal of Industrial Economics*, Vol. XXIII, June, (1975).

Kamerschen, D.R. "The Influence of Ownership and Control on Profit Rates". *American Economic Review*, Vol. 58, (1968).

Katrak, H. "Cost-Price Relationship in India Manufacturing Industries". *The Journal of Development Studies*, 17, (1980).

Knight, Frank. *Risk, Uncertainty and Profit.* Houghton Hiffin Company, Boston and New York, 1934.

Kuznets, Simon. *Capital in the American Economy; Its Formation and Financing.* Princeton University Press, 1961.

Larner, R.J. "Ownership and Control in the 200 Largest Non-Financial Corporations, 1929 and 1963". *American Economic Review*, September, (1966).

Lenin, V.I. *Collected Works.* Vol. 24.

Mann, H.M. "Seller Concentration, Barriers to Entry and Rates of Return in 30 Industries, 1950-69". *Review of Economics and Statistics*, 48, (1966).

Marris, Robin. *The Economic Theory of Managerial Capitatism.* Macmillan Company, London, 1964.

McEachern, William. "Corporate Control and Growth: An Alternative Approach". *The Journal of Industrial Economics*, March, (1978).

Meade, J.E. "In the New Industrial State Inevitable". *Economic Journal*, June, (1968).

Modigliani and Miller. "The Cost of Capital, Corporation Finance and the Theory of Investment." *American Economic Review*, June, (1958).

Monsen, Chiu and Colley." The Effect of Separation of Ownership And Control On the Performance of the Large Firm." *Quartely Journal of Economics*, August,

(1968).

Radica, H.K. "Control Type, Profitability and Growth in Large Firms. An Empirical Study." *The Economic Journal*, Vol. 81, September, (1971).

Samuels, J. and Smith, D. "Profits, Variability of Profits and Firm Size". *Economica*, 35, (1968).

Sawhney, P. and Sawhney, B. "Capacity Utilisation, Concentration and Price - Cost Margins. Results on Indian Industries". *Journal of Industrial Economics*, 21, (1973).

Schumpeter, Joseph. *The Theory of Economic Development.* Harvard University Press, Cambridge, 1934.

Schwartzman, David. "Effect of Monopoly on Price." *Journal of Political Economy*, 67, (1959).

Singh, Ajit. *Takeover.* Cambridge, 1971.

Singh and Whittington. *Growth, Profitability and Valuation.* Cambridge, 1968.

Sorensen, Robert. "The Separation of Ownership and Control and Firm Performance." *Southern Economic Journal*, Vol. 41, July, (1974).

Stekler, H.O. *Profitability and Size of Firm.* Berkeley, 1963.

Stigler, G.J. *Capital and Rates of Returns in Manufacturing Industries.* Princeton University Press, 1963.

Thanyavur. "Companies Act Amendment Bill." *Economic and Political Weekly*, December 26th, (1987).

Thonet and Poensgen. "Managerial Control and Economic Performance in Western Germany." *The Journal of Industrial Economics*, September, (1979).

Tungendhat, Christopher. *The Multinationals.* Pelican, 1978.

Williamsons, O.E. *The Economics of Discretionary Behaviour*, New Jersey, 1964.

Index

ABOUT THE AUTHOR :

Dr. Malay K. Roy (Faculty of Commerce, University of North Bengal, India) has a long experience of teaching Post-graduate classes as well as guiding research in the areas of Financial Management and Investment Management. Dr. Roy has completed several research projects sponsored by Government and semi-government bodies and actively participated in a number of national and international seminars and has published several research papers in academic and professional Journals. Presently he is working on Indian Stock Market studies.